Praise for Geoff Hill's previous book, *The Battle for Zimbabwe*

'Mr. Hill succeeds where few other writers have. His book is meticulously researched and fearless, and the best of its kind.'

– Professor Amir Attaran, Faculty of Law, University of Ottawa, Canada

'Geoff Hill does a superb job in giving the background on how Mugabe has manipulated his grip on power, and in the process destroyed the political and economic fabric of a nation.'

– Walter Kansteiner, US Assistant Secretary of State for Africa 2000–2004, Washington

'*The Battle for Zimbabwe* is essential reading for any follower of Southern African politics and a stark reminder of the tragedy that is unfolding in Zimbabwe.'

– Kerry Sibraa, AO, president of the Australian senate 1987–1994; Australian high commissioner to Zimbabwe 1994–1998

'Geoff Hill tells the story of a country being strangled by a tyrannical regime masquerading as a legitimate government where freedom and democracy have been replaced by violence and starvation. A cold reminder of South Africa's impotence in addressing a situation which is fast escalating into chaos.'

– Kaajal Ramjathan, human rights attorney, Lawyers for Human Rights, Johannesburg

'*The Battle for Zimbabwe* is a captivating story about the struggle for freedom long after Zimbabwe attained independence. Written by an expert with a finger on the country's political pulse, even those familiar with the events find it highly informative.'

– Geoffrey Nyarota, founding editor, *Daily News*

'Hill takes the reader inside Robert Mugabe's party, Zanu-PF, and the opposition MDC. Members of both parties talk candidly with him, giving him behind-the-scenes information.'

– Editors' Choice, *News 24*

'Hill has produced a record of events that will keep alive the consequences of misrule. Hopefully it will help prevent deviant behaviour from developing elsewhere and also help to bring to book those who can still be held to account.'

– Zimbabwe Independent

'Geoff Hill's *The Battle for Zimbabwe: The Final Countdown*, is the most realistic attempt yet to chart the troubled times of that country.'

– Barry Baxter, *Marung*

'This is a book that should be read by everyone in South Africa as a warning of what can happen if we allow apathy to dilute the strength of our own fledgling democracy, as well as being a damning indictment of the so-called "quiet diplomacy" being practiced by our own rulers.'

– Peter Canavan, *Pretoria News*

WHAT HAPPENS AFTER MUGABE?

GEOFF HILL

Published by Zebra Press
an imprint of Struik Publishers
(a division of New Holland Publishing (South Africa) (Pty) Ltd)
PO Box 1144, Cape Town, 8000
New Holland Publishing is a member of Avusa Ltd

www.zebrapress.co.za

First published 2005
Reprinted in 2005, 2006, 2007(twice) and 2008

7 9 10 8 6

PUBLISHING MANAGER: Marlene Fryer
MANAGING EDITOR: Robert Plummer
EDITOR: Marléne Burger
PROOFREADER: Ronel Richter-Herbert
COVER AND TEXT DESIGNER: Natascha Adendorff-Olivier
TYPESETTER: Monique van den Berg
PRODUCTION MANAGER: Valerie Kömmer

Set in 10 pt on 13.7 pt Plantin Light

Reproduction by Hirt & Carter (Cape) (Pty) Ltd
Printed and bound by Paarl Print, Oosterland Street, Paarl, South Africa

ISBN 978 1 77007 102 5

Contents

To all who struggle to be free

Preface

ON 31 MARCH 2005, ROBERT MUGABE AND HIS RULING ZANU-PF party claimed victory in an election marred by a voters' roll years out of date and a state-controlled media that not only favoured the government, but pumped out hate speech against the opposition Movement for Democratic Change (MDC).

The police, army and youth militia had waged a five-year campaign of violence against the population, and widespread hunger left many dependent on food handouts, which, they were told, would be denied 'to those who do not vote wisely'.

As if that wasn't enough, there were allegations of outright rigging.

Predictably, most Western nations dismissed the vote as a fraud, and Mugabe's win brought him no closer to the international recognition he needed if Zimbabwe was to shed its pariah status and enjoy the aid, trade and rebuilding required to pull it out of the *Guinness Book of Records*, where it held top place for the world's highest inflation and fastest-shrinking economy.

But, what was more interesting than the election itself was Mugabe's campaign, which centred on regime change. To a casual observer, it might have seemed that the eighty-one-year-old president was standing against British prime minister Tony Blair.

In speech after speech, Mugabe denigrated Blair and US president George W Bush, telling voters that 'these two monsters' were the real enemy, not opposition leader Morgan Tsvangirai and his Movement for Democratic Change.

'Bush and Blair want to make Zimbabwe their own,' he told a rally in the southern province of Matabeleland days before the poll, 'and they want their puppet Tsvangirai in power. They are determined to effect regime change, but they will be defeated.'

It was political nonsense, but Mugabe had little else to offer: unemployment stood at 90 per cent, a third of the population had gone into exile, and millions were hungry in a country that, until recently, had grown enough crops to feed itself and much of southern Africa.

Ironically, the 'enemies' that cropped up most frequently in his speeches – Britain, the US, Canada, Australia, New Zealand and the nations of Scandinavia – were former allies that, in the 1980s, had stood silent while he murdered thousands and built a political system of which the sole purpose was to keep himself and his party in power.

But, while it was laughable to suggest that a Western alliance was planning to topple Mugabe after the fashion of the Taliban or Saddam Hussein, it was clear that, on the world stage at least, Mr Mugabe had outstayed his welcome:

- Zimbabwe had been ousted from the Commonwealth.
- Mugabe and his ministers were banned from visiting Europe and the United States.
- Their assets in those countries had been frozen.
- Donor funds were being used to assist those working for change both at home and among exile groups around the globe.

But, while many wanted Mugabe to go – not least his own people – few had considered the task that would lie ahead once democracy had taken hold and those who had ruined the country were pushed from office.

Since 1990, Africa has undergone a revolution as long-time leaders, under pressure to reform, let go of their one-party states and military dictatorships and held multiparty elections. But, where change came, it was often so fast that, before much good could be done, a new elite had entrenched themselves as solidly in power as those they had replaced.

In Zambia, Malawi and Kenya, parties that had ruled since the early 1960s were voted out, but a lack of preparation meant that corruption endured, and often grew worse, while the new governments did little to tackle poverty and unemployment. Tellingly, exile populations driven out by past regimes stayed abroad, and the brain drain continued as those who felt betrayed by a new revolution gone astray left home, robbing the country of much-needed skills.

Yet, despite those lessons, by 2005, seven years after it became clear that time was running out for Mugabe and the old guard who kept him in power, donor nations and NGOs had not drawn up plans for a new Zimbabwe. Instead, there seemed to be a notion that, if only the bad guys would go, the spirit of Mother Teresa would descend from heaven and guide the new rulers as they set about creating a paradise, where people would live in joy to the end of days.

This book was originally planned as a newspaper story, but as the research progressed, I realised how little there was to go on. Many events and conversations gave me an insight into what lies ahead for the country, but two encounters convinced me to turn my proposed article into a book.

In 2004, I interviewed Ambassador Andy Bearpark, CBE, who had worked as the European Union's representative in post-war Kosovo, where he was also the UN secretary general's deputy special representative. After the fall of Saddam Hussein, he was put in charge of Iraq's reconstruction, reporting directly to US administrator Paul Bremer. But, most importantly for me,

Andy had been part of the British government's aid team to post-war Zimbabwe in the 1980s.

He is now regarded as one of the world's leading authorities on reconstruction, and at a ninety-minute meeting, he gave me a list of questions I would need to ask others more closely associated with Zimbabwe.

'Each case is different,' he told me over tea at a small hotel near his home in rural England. 'But there are two constants: rebuilding a country is always more difficult than people think, and everything comes down to planning and preparation.

'Governments worry that if they pay for plans and then the event doesn't come to pass, they have wasted their money. But it is cheaper – much cheaper – to draw up blueprints that aren't used than to go into a country without plans and try to put things right.'

On the subject of cost, he said that rebuilding always took more money than expected. Infrastructure had to be restored, food imported, business and agriculture revived, skilled exiles had to be wooed home and encouraged to stay and not to go about settling scores with those who had forced them to leave.

And while all this was happening, the government had to busy itself building democracy, freeing up the media and handling the crises that are part of running any country, but more so in a hurting and fragile land. In Andy's experience, new problems arose from the very act of rebuilding.

> Things break down slowly, bit by bit, and only when you start to fix the problem do you realise how shambolic it really is.
>
> I often use the analogy of a student's car with rough gears and no handbrake. The student drives it every day and knows which gears stick, when to pump the clutch and that you have to put a brick under the wheel if you park on a slope.

> Then someone else buys the vehicle, knowing that it's far from new but not aware of the exact problems. And, in a day, the new owner has wrecked the car.
>
> This is what happens when donor countries and their experts come in to fix a country. The people running the system know how to keep it going, but a lot of damage can be done once you start putting things right.
>
> You can just about keep power stations going if you know where the faults are. But once they collapse completely, then, like a car that's been written off, you have to start again from scratch.
>
> Now, with the power station, you have to take the whole plant out of service and rebuild it. So, whereas there used to be cuts, there is no power at all and people say that the old regime was better and Western donors throw up their hands, amazed that anyone could think that.

We worked through the other essentials, including a free media, strong protection of human rights, a good constitution and an independent judiciary, none of which existed under Mugabe.

'But remember this,' Andy said, as we closed. 'People need to feel they are part of the process, otherwise even good moves may be resisted by the public, because they see the change as something that is being imposed on them.'

A few weeks later, I was in Rwanda with the faculty of human rights law from the University of Pretoria. I had been a guest lecturer for their master's degree programme, discussing the common ethics that should guide both writers and lawyers, such as confidentiality of sources, and the careful handling of people who have been tortured or abused. Too often, when deadlines are pressing, journalists can add to a victim's trauma by pushing for detail when the teller is clearly finding it hard to relive the experience in words. In the trade we refer to this kind of bullying as, 'Anyone here been raped and speak English?'

The faculty is led by Norman Taku from Cameroon and Martin Nsibirwa, who hails from Uganda. Both knew Rwanda from past excursions, and each of the twenty-six students, all from different countries in Africa, brought their own ideas and experiences. Adding to the mix was David Padilla, a visiting lecturer from the US, with a good knowledge of human rights from his time in South and Central America.

We toured sites of the genocide, heard stories from survivors, viewed tens of thousands of skulls and other bones, still unburied, and probed officials from the Rwandan government and the UN tribunal in charge of the war crimes trials. As we asked our questions and shared our notes, the trip soon became a journey of learning for teachers and students alike, and especially for me.

I have dealt with the 1994 genocide in the book, but what amazed me was how Rwanda came through it, building a better and stronger country within a decade.

Not for a moment would I equate Mugabe with the killers who took the lives of 800 000 Rwandans in just 100 days. Yes, in the 1980s, Mugabe did commit genocide in Matabeland, but even the highest estimates put the number of dead at 40 000. But for thirty years before the madness in Rwanda, the country had been misgoverned – again, to a far greater degree than Zimbabwe – yet in spite of this and the massacres, the new leaders have turned it into a place that works.

The capital, Kigali, is a delightful town with clean streets, power, good phones and a charm that begs you to return. Tourists come mostly to see gorillas in the Virunga Mountains, three hours by road from Kigali and hell's own climb, but worth the trip.

Recently, the new government of Paul Kagame has shown worrying signs of intolerance: the media is under check, there have been political disappearances and a democratic future is far from certain. But Kagame has rebuilt Rwanda in a way that can only inspire those who know how badly these things have been handled elsewhere in Africa.

Sadly, at every step he was hampered by a lack of planning. Few, it seemed, had given any thought to the idea that the previous one-party state might be toppled by its own people.

By now I had decided to turn my planned article into a book, and I am indebted to many people who helped me with the task. Ian Fleming once said that writing a book was as much fun as digging a very deep hole, but, in my case, the work was made lighter and better by those who have given so freely of their time, often recounting memories they would rather forget.

It is five years since I was commissioned to write *The Battle for Zimbabwe*, and in the course of that work and this shorter text, I have interviewed nearly 1 400 people, some alone, others in groups or forums. Each had his or her view on how things got so bad, what could be done to right the problem and how to make sure it doesn't happen again.

In the words of Ernest Hemingway, my only task was to put what I heard, saw and felt on paper 'in the best and simplest way'.

Special thanks go to my publishers, Steve Connolly and Marlene Fryer, editors Robert Plummer, Marléne Burger and Ronel Richter-Herbert, and to Natascha Adendorff and Nick Russell who, between them, came up with the cover. My appreciation also to Barnaby Phillips, who perused the final text; to Neil Higgs and Research Surveys, who carried out the opinion polls used in the epilogue; and to Dr Len Weinstein and his staff who, in treating the many torture victims I brought to their rooms, gave hope and healing to those who had paid a terrible price in their fight for justice.

Books on tyranny and its aftermath can be depressing and there is sombre detail in this one, but also uplifting stories of survival and dreams for the future, plus reports on countries like Mali, Chile, South Africa and Somaliland that have come out of hard times and built a new order.

An activist once told me that her second greatest fear for Zimbabwe was five more years of rule by Mugabe's ZANU-PF party. Her greatest anxiety centred on change that might come before anyone had planned what would happen next. 'Some people are so focused on change itself, they become like a dog chasing a car,' she said. 'Lots of noise and energy, but the dog would have no idea what to do if it caught one.'

One only has to look at the democratic change that has taken place in Eastern Europe, South and Central America, and in South Africa to see that history is not on the side of those who won the 2005 election, and there is no doubt that freedom will come to Zimbabwe, even if we can't put a date on it. And, when that happens, will Britain, the US and others who took a stand against Mugabe come up with the money and programmes needed to rebuild the nation – not just to repair the decay, but to create new structures to protect democracy and ensure that the same tragedy never happens again?

In February 2005, on her first trip abroad as US Secretary of State, Condoleezza Rice used a line that will long be quoted for its truth and poignancy.

'History does not just happen,' she told an audience at the Institut d'Études Politique in Paris. 'History is made by men and women of conviction, of commitment and of courage, who will not let their dreams be denied.'

Zimbabwe has no shortage of such people, and they deserve our help in making sure that what happens after Mugabe stands as an example to other nations that have struggled to be free.

GEOFF HILL

MAY 2005

1

State of Decay

When a group has entrenched itself in power, then it regards its rights and privileges as sacrosanct. – Robert Mugabe

IT WAS HARD NOT TO FEEL SORRY FOR GIDEON GONO, governor of the Reserve Bank of Zimbabwe. He had been trying to speak for the past ten minutes, but couldn't make himself heard over the insults.

'Go back to Zimbabwe!'

'Soon we will put you on trial!'

'You are Mugabe's dog, go and chew bones!'

Zimbabwe's ambassador to South Africa, Simon Kaya Moyo, stayed seated at the end of the VIP table, facing the hall of protesters. Security officers were on hand, but realising they were outnumbered they merely guarded the doors and steered clear of the mob.

Gono patted the air, signalling the crowd to hush, but instead they pulled raw eggs from their pockets and threw them at the speaker.

It was close to 7 p.m. on Saturday 12 June 2004, and the Zimbabwean legation had rented a posh hall halfway between South Africa's largest city, Johannesburg, and the capital, Pretoria. A sixty-kilometre highway links the two, but over the years farms along the route have given way to suburbs and light industrial sites to create an almost unbroken urban sprawl.

Near the thirty-kilometre peg, in an area known as Midrand, a cluster of halls and convention centres offers the chance to stage anything from a national expo to a private party. And it was here that Ambassador Moyo was hosting Dr Gono, who had also been a financial advisor to President Robert Mugabe. The octogenarian leader had been in power since independence in 1980, and was rumoured to have plundered Zimbabwe's national coffers and stashed the spoils in Malaysia. If that was true, the chances were that Dr Gono was privy to some of the deals.

But on this trip, he was pleading for money to flow *into* Zimbabwe.

Just five years earlier the country had been a major exporter, but repression and misrule had led to the collapse of the agricultural, mining and tourism sectors. As a result, money sent home by exiles was now the largest source of foreign earnings.

One third of the total population of 13 million had fled the country, and the Pretoria government's data indicated that by the end of 2004, South Africa had become home to 3 million black Zimbabweans, with hundreds more crossing the border every day.

On the face of it, a growing diaspora would increase the flow of money back home, but it wasn't that simple. Gono – on orders from Mugabe – had pegged the Zimbabwe dollar at an unrealistic exchange rate, so if the exiles sent cash through banks or Western Union, their families received a pittance in local currency.

In response, an army of money changers had sprung up in London and Johannesburg, offering better rates and a one-hour service: hand over your foreign cash here, and Zimbabwe dollars will be paid into the recipient's bank account almost immediately. No trace, no forms, no hassle and no foreign exchange coming through the Treasury in Harare.

'Please, just hear what we want to tell you and then you can make your protest,' Gono pleaded.

'Take your ambassador and go before we hang you both!'

The meeting had started out well enough. The protesters – mostly in their middle to late twenties – had gathered in orderly fashion outside the hall. Some wore shirts promoting the opposition Movement for Democratic Change (MDC), and there had been a delay while Moyo and Gono debated whether or not to cancel the event in case of trouble.

They decided to continue, and embassy officials handed out free T-shirts advertising the legal cash transfer procedure known as Homelink. People smiled and joked as they donned the garments over their clothes and filed quietly into the auditorium.

A head table had been prepared for the VIPs, complete with food and drink, and both the ambassador and the governor must have been delighted that so many had chosen to attend the meeting. But a closer look at the crowd would have shown that everyone was pregnant, or so it appeared from the bulging tummies of men and women alike.

As soon as the governor started speaking, his audience rose, as if for an ovation, but it wasn't applause that came from the floor. Instead, people reached under their clothes and removed the bulges, which turned out to be black T-shirts emblazoned with red and yellow text reading: 'Free Zimbabwe! Mugabe Must Go!'

Undaunted – or perhaps in shock – Gono carried on talking and even raised his voice, but the loudspeakers were no match for the noise from the floor. From the back of the hall one could see that Gono's lips were moving, but it was impossible to hear him.

'We don't want Homelink, give us Votelink!' someone shouted, and the crowd took up the chant: 'Votelink not Homelink! Votelink not Homelink!'

Some two years earlier the Zimbabwe government had abolished absentee voting for nationals living abroad, and clearly it was still a sore point.

With a wail of sirens the police arrived and pushed into the crowd, but made no effort to restore order. Instead, they formed a line between the exiles and the ambassador and his guests. Out of eggs, the crowd began ripping up their Homelink T-shirts and lobbing balls of cloth at Gono.

Five minutes later the governor and his ambassador left the building and were swept away in a chauffeur-driven Mercedes, while the victors cheered, sang, danced and cleared the VIP table of food and wine.

Still the police did not intervene, except to say that the hall should be empty by 8 p.m., when the dog squad would be sent in. Sated and singing, the exiles left at 7.45, begging lifts home to the slums where they lived in crowded squalor.

Simon Kaya Moyo was no stranger to protest, and had watched dozens of demonstrations outside his embassy in Pretoria when the Zimbabweans he was there to serve called for the mission to be closed on account of what they alleged was Mugabe's poor record on human rights.

Gideon Gono had also received his share of brickbats, having travelled to South Africa from London, where he had tried to address similar meetings, only to be shouted down. He did, however, manage to get his message across at a number of closed forums.

The anger channelled against these two men who are, in themselves, both decent human beings, is typical when people feel they have been abused by their government: South Africans in exile during apartheid; East Timorese living in Australia while their country was occupied by Indonesia; millions of Afghans crowded into camps across the border in Pakistan during the Soviet occupation in the 1980s and under the Taliban a decade later.

Through these small victories, exiles sustain their morale, stoking the hope that soon the tyrants will be toppled and free elections will usher in a new government, anxious to serve the needs of a willing electorate.

Come that day, from their places of asylum around the globe, political and economic refugees will go home to enjoy the rights that American revolutionary Thomas Jefferson described as 'life, liberty and the pursuit of happiness'.

But, all too often, reality falls short of the dream.

In Africa, Asia and the Middle East, more than a hundred governments have been overthrown since 1960, but in most cases the new regimes have been little better, sometimes worse, and rarely democratic.

The list is long: Burma, Laos, Vietnam, Pakistan, Iran, Somalia, Burundi, Libya, Sudan, Eritrea, Ethiopia and the Congo all saw regime change at gunpoint, yet by 2005 not one of them had a truly free press or democratic space for loyal opposition, and all had significant exile populations living around the world.

Even in countries where America and its allies oversaw the revolution, the results were depressing. In Afghanistan, the Taliban regime was removed by force in 2001, but in the wake of liberation, hardly a day goes by without explosions and sniper fire, and the country remains one of the poorest on earth.

Iraq fared little better, and as the death toll continues to rise and the position of ordinary citizens remains dire, one cannot help but wonder whether the money spent on deposing Saddam Hussein and propping up the new regime might not have been put to better effect wiping out malaria in Africa and Asia, and building schools and improving life for the more than 1.2 billion people around the world who survive on less than $1 a day.[1]

The cost of the second Iraq war – excluding the subsequent occupation and reconstruction – is more than $125 billion, enough to fund all the world's hunger programmes for five years, supply drugs to every AIDS patient for a decade, put 17 million children through a year of pre-school, or immunise every child on the planet against infant diseases for half a century.[2]

US and British troops did not find the weapons of mass destruction that President George W Bush and Prime Minister Tony Blair had used as a pretext for invading Iraq, but there was no shortage of evidence that Saddam had committed enough heinous crimes to justify his overthrow. Huge rooms were discovered filled with instruments of torture; thousands of political prisoners were killed during his reign; and in August 1990 he invaded neighbouring Kuwait and overthrew the government. When forced to retreat, his troops set fire to that country's oil wells.

But his worst offence was to obliterate hundreds of Kurdish villages in retribution for their inhabitants siding with neighbouring Iran against Iraq during the 1980s. Estimates of how many Kurds were killed on Saddam's orders range from 50 000 to 180 000. Survivors were bombed and gassed as they fled the genocide.[3] Many Iraqi Kurds were left blind by the mustard gas, and a decade later birth defects are still common in children whose parents were attacked with chemical weapons.[4]

If one could wave a magic wand and restore Saddam Hussein to power, surely no rational person would wish such a fate on the people of Iraq? But the point is that, even with a virtually unlimited budget and the backing of great democracies like Britain, Australia and the USA, bringing freedom to a country takes much more than simply getting rid of despots like Saddam ... or Mugabe.

There have, of course, been exceptions. Since the advent of democracy in 1994, South Africa has enjoyed more freedom than any country in the history of the continent.

Chile, which until 1990 was under the military rule of General Augusto Pinochet, not only became democratic, but performs well economically. In the five years to 2003, imports remained steady, while exports rose almost 30 per cent to $21 billion.[5] And long-time basket cases like Nigeria, Mozambique and Zambia look set to improve as new leaders do their best to heal decades of theft and neglect. But in Zimbabwe, the challenges loom especially large.

In February 1980, when Mugabe was declared prime minister, and in South Africa when Nelson Mandela assumed power in 1994, strong economies existed in both countries, capable of bearing the strain of transition. Post-Mugabe, it is not just a lack of capacity that would stand in the way of progress. In Zimbabwe:

- Law and order has broken down and the police are politicised.
- Inflation is the highest in the world.
- Nine out of ten adults are unemployed.
- The state-run youth militia has set up a terror network across the nation.
- Commercial farming has collapsed, and food agencies estimate that 75 per cent of the population doesn't have enough to eat.
- There is virtually no public health system.
- A shortage of teachers has crippled the school system.
- Between 25 and 33 per cent of the population is in exile.
- Between 70 and 90 per cent of all university graduates are believed to be working outside the country.

So, when freedom comes, is there a chance that Zimbabwe can reclaim its place as Africa's second most viable economy? Before seeking answers, we need to look at how the tragedy came about and review some of the tasks that would face a future government.

'It's all about power and the abuse of office,' human rights lawyer Gabriel Shumba told me when I asked him to summarise the problems in his country. Gabriel had fled Zimbabwe after being interrogated by the feared secret police, known as the Central Intelligence Organisation or CIO, which operates from Mugabe's office. He had been working as a lawyer in Harare and was preparing a case against the government on behalf of an opposition member of parliament, Job Sikhala, who had been tortured by the CIO.

On 14 January 2003, Gabriel was talking to Sikhala in Harare when police broke into his office and took them both into custody. Over the next three days, Gabriel was beaten, hung upside down for hours on end, and tortured with electric shocks to his feet, mouth and genitals. In the end he was charged under the notorious Public Order and Security Act (POSA), and acquitted. Still under threat of death, he fled to South Africa and became a tutor in human rights law at the University of Pretoria.

It was 6°C on a winter morning as we sat huddled over our mugs at a coffee bar in Pretoria and he told me his thoughts on why Zimbabwe had landed in such a mess.

> The world looked the other way when Mugabe took over in 1980, because so many eminent people had staked their reputations on this man. Mugabe had risen to power in the nationalist movement by collaborating in the murder and intimidation of anyone who stood in his way, and long before the British government handed the country to him on a platter at independence in 1980 it was clear to anyone who cared to scan the evidence that the man was a thug.
>
> Leaders with otherwise impeccable credentials, like Malcolm Fraser (then prime minister of Australia), Jimmy Carter and Andrew Young in America, Brian Mulroney of Canada, all the leaders of the Scandinavian countries and almost the entire British parliament kept quiet as Mugabe nationalised the press, committed genocide against minority tribes and subverted our country's constitution to make himself the sole source of authority.

> Twenty years on, the people had suffered enough and formed a new party that had the capacity to defeat Mugabe in the 2000 general elections.
>
> It was then that he confiscated almost all white farmland, promising to hand it out to blacks if they voted for him. But Zimbabwe today is an educated and increasingly urban society, with no use for land. People want jobs, and instead Mugabe has delivered 90 per cent unemployment. It is this and his human rights record that have driven people into exile.

I was writing as fast as I could while taking sips of coffee and warming my hands on the mug so that I could hold my pen. While I caught up with the text and verified some of the details, Gabriel ordered doughnuts, and we spent a while chatting about life.

At thirty, he was almost young enough to be my son, but seemed older than his years; not just mature, but wearied by the pain he had endured, his body young and straight but his spirit stooped by the horror of it all.

We ate our doughnuts as the morning air warmed around us. The South African Highveld has a crisp, dry winter, with blue skies and a pale sun, void of power. In summer – from November to April – Pretoria can hit 34°C at midday, and the nights are balmy. Gabriel suddenly continued:

> It's been like an endless winter in Zimbabwe. People are waiting for some miracle to bring life back to the land, but all they see is hunger and misery; Mugabe and his cronies flash past in new Mercedes, while others have had to sell their donkeys just to put food on the table. Taking the land away from commercial farmers was the last straw, because now the country is starving.
>
> Mugabe and his ministers have grabbed the best farms

> and they use them as weekend retreats and don't grow anything. The rest of the land lies empty. Our white commercial farmers have been snatched away by countries like Mozambique, Malawi, Zambia and Nigeria, which couldn't believe their luck.'

If some nations have a rich history, the story of Zimbabwe over the past 200 years is enough to make you bilious: so many events crammed together, with little time for people to learn from the recent past before the next wave of change came rolling in.

The human history of the land between the Zambezi River in the north and the Limpopo to the south dates back perhaps 100 000 years, and for 99 per cent of that time only one people occupied the region. The Bushmen, or San – short, slightly built aborigines – hunted game and gathered seeds and fruits.

When the herds moved on, so did they, sheltering in caves where they decorated the stone walls with paintings of the world around them – zebra, buffalo, eland, lion, elephant, sometimes even pictures of themselves hunting, dancing and making love. In a cave near Rusape, the famous sketch called Diana's Vow is almost pornographic – clearly the San knew how to throw an orgy.

Women gave birth every year, but had no defence against malaria and other tropical ailments, and few children reached maturity. But it was a successful culture and, over time, the San spread across present-day Zimbabwe, living in harmony with nature and, no doubt, believing themselves to be the only people on earth.

Around AD 900, ancestors of the Shona people, who now make up 70 per cent of Zimbabwe's population, moved south from the Great Lakes region near Burundi and Rwanda, bringing herds of cattle and tilling the savannah to plant indigenous grains, which they reaped and stored.

By AD 1000 they had crossed the Zambezi, and over the next 800 years the Shona colonised the region, displacing the San and taking the land for crops and grazing. The Shona were an astute and industrious people, and somewhere around 1200 they built a stone fortress in the central-southern part of the country. From there a succession of kings, known as the Monomotapa, ruled a great civilisation, trading gold, slaves and ivory with merchants from the Middle East.

The ruined city of Zimbabwe – from which the modern nation takes its name – can still be seen near the town of Masvingo, 250 kilometres south of Harare. By 1500, the kingdom had been torn apart by infighting and overpopulation and the city deserted, but life for the Shona was still rich, with no one to challenge their dominance.

More than a thousand kilometres away, on the south-east coast of Africa, turmoil broke out in 1820 when Shaka became king of the Zulu nation and subdued the neighbouring tribes. Like Alexander the Great he had a gift for strategy, and soon much of the present-day South African province of KwaZulu-Natal fell under his rule.

When one of Shaka's generals, Mzilikazi, fell out with the king in 1828, he fled north, setting up temporary bases along the way and conquering local tribes, whose numbers he added to his own. In 1840 he built a permanent home for his people – who had taken the name amaNdebele – near what is now Zimbabwe's southern city of Bulawayo.

For the next fifty years, Mzilikazi and his heir, Lobengula, slaughtered the Shona, stole their cattle and conquered most of the territory that forms modern Zimbabwe. From the 1850s, missionaries and prospectors began exploring the region, and tales emerged of a fertile land, rich in gold. The first claim was true, but dreams of mineral wealth sprang from the discovery of old mines and the ruined city of Zimbabwe.

In 1890, lured by these stories, British-born diamond magnate Cecil John Rhodes commissioned a pioneer column of white settlers to move into Matabeleland.

Rhodes tricked Lobengula into a treaty, but when war broke out with the Matabele, and later between white settlers and the Shona, the black rebellions were put down with brute force, and by 1900 the country was under control of Rhodes's British South Africa Company.

The new government stopped the Matabele from raiding the Shona, and established an administrative system of district commissioners, along with a police force and army, both of which were dominated by blacks but commanded by whites.

The majority of Shona and Matabele cattle were confiscated and handed to the settlers, and the best land was cut up into farms.

Rhodes died in 1902, and in 1923 Rhodesia, named in his honour, was granted special status by the British government as the empire's first self-governing colony, putting it almost on a par with the dominion states of Canada, Australia, New Zealand and South Africa.

Waves of British immigrants – and others from Greece, Portugal, France and South Africa – boosted the white population, and by 1960 Rhodesia was home to more than 200 000 whites … and 2 million blacks.

The harsh apartheid policies of South Africa never made it across the Limpopo, but Rhodesia was not a just society. While the university and private schools were mixed, government schools were segregated by race, as were hospitals, suburbs and even the rural areas. The black population had exclusive access to half the country and lived in their own townships in the cities, but they could not buy land or homes in white areas, and vice versa.

In 1953 the country joined in federation with Northern

Rhodesia (now Zambia) and Nyasaland (now Malawi), but the grouping was broken up at the end of 1962, and Britain granted independence to Zambia and Malawi.

The Rhodesians demanded their own sovereignty, but London insisted that there should first be black majority rule. Technically, any Rhodesian over the age of eighteen with a certain level of education and property rights could vote, but in reality the system favoured the white minority.

On 11 November 1965, frustrated by the drawn-out negotiations with the government of Harold Wilson, Rhodesian prime minister Ian Smith became only the second leader in history to declare his country independent from Britain. The first was George Washington in 1776.

The only countries to offer tacit recognition of Rhodesia's Unilateral Declaration of Independence, or UDI, were South Africa, under a white apartheid government, and Portugal, which still ruled Mozambique and Angola. South Africa in particular cooperated with the new state and helped Smith to bypass United Nations sanctions, which had been imposed at the request of Britain.

The Rhodesian economy diversified, and it seemed as if white rule might continue indefinitely. That is, until black nationalist leaders, eager to take charge and angry at continued discrimination, went into exile in 1972 and established guerrilla bases in neighbouring states. The fighters, armed with landmines, rifles and grenades, infiltrated Rhodesia, and for eight years the country was locked in civil war.

In 1976, Smith conceded to the principle of one person, one vote, and in April 1979 the first democratic elections returned Bishop Abel Muzorewa as the new black prime minister. The two guerrilla leaders, Mugabe and Joshua Nkomo, refused to contest the poll.

But the country, now known as Zimbabwe-Rhodesia, was

on its knees, short of money, manpower and weapons, and conducting an all-out war against Nkomo's mostly Matabele forces based in Zambia, and Mugabe's Shona army, which operated from Mozambique.

Muzorewa launched operations deep into Mozambique and Zambia, weakening the enemy and cutting their supplies of Russian and Chinese weapons coming up from the coast, but no side was close to victory. Military experts agreed that the war would drag on for years unless a political solution was found.

At the end of 1979, the new Conservative government of Margaret Thatcher hosted peace talks in London, and her foreign secretary, Lord Peter Carrington, managed to convince Mugabe, Nkomo and Muzorewa that each had a chance of winning new elections.

Under the accord, the guerrillas moved into holding camps inside Rhodesia, but Mugabe sent local collaborators to the assembly points, while many of his soldiers remained at large, intimidating voters into supporting his party at the polls. But even if he had played by the rules, it was clear that Mugabe had the numbers, if only because voters saw him as the only man capable of ending the war that had wrought such misery on their lives.

The British-sponsored election took place in February 1980, and Mugabe's Zimbabwe African National Union-Patriotic Front (ZANU-PF) won fifty-six of the eighty seats. Nkomo's Zimbabwe African People's Union (ZAPU) took twenty, Muzorewa managed just three, and veteran nationalist, the Reverend Ndabaningi Sithole, held only one seat, in his home area of Chipinge.

On 18 April 1980, the Republic of Zimbabwe gained formal independence from Britain.

Mugabe pledged himself to reconciliation, but by the next election in 1985 he had nationalised the press, extended his own powers and sent the specially trained, all-Shona Fifth Brigade into Matabeleland, where between 8 000 and 40 000 of Nkomo's supporters were murdered and thousands more tortured in southern Africa's only modern-day genocide, which became known as *Gukurahundi*, a Shona term for the wind that blows away the chaff after harvest.

In 1987, with his home province in ruins, Nkomo dissolved his party and merged with ZANU-PF. The office of prime minister was scrapped, Mugabe became president with new powers that allowed him to virtually rule by decree, and Nkomo accepted the largely ceremonial post of vice-president.

Zimbabwe entered a decade of uneasy peace in which every aspect of daily life was controlled in some way by ZANU-PF. Through a system of patronage, Mugabe rewarded loyalty by appointing his allies to jobs in the public service, local government, the media and an extensive network of parastatals.

In Rhodesian days, the government had promoted black education. Now, to his credit, Mugabe – a teacher by profession – pumped millions of dollars into schools, and within a decade Zimbabwe had the best-educated population in Africa. However, no provision was made for the needs of an educated workforce.

In the twenty years from 1980, Zimbabwe's population almost doubled to 12 million, but over the same period Harare grew fivefold as young people with literacy levels better than those in some of Britain's government schools left their parents' traditional lifestyle centred on crops and cattle, and moved to the city.

The trend was not unusual: studies in Thailand, Brazil, Kenya and the Philippines have shown that, when rural people gain an education, they invariably move to town in search of a better life.

Across Zimbabwe, urban unemployment rose dramatically as, year after year, schools and universities pushed more graduates into the job market, where fewer than one in four people was in formal employment.

The first riots – sparked largely by the unions – erupted in 1997, and by 2000 polling showed that voters were ready to throw ZANU-PF out of office.

In February 2000, Mugabe offered his people a chance to alter the constitution through a referendum. Under the new deal, vast tracts of fertile land owned by Zimbabwe's 4 000 white commercial farmers would be seized and redistributed among landless blacks. A plan to spread ownership more evenly had been drawn up after independence and was funded from London, until it emerged that farms bought from whites were being given to black government ministers and their families.

Britain and other donors withdrew from the scheme, but now the government would take the land without compensation.

The new deal would also limit the head of state to two terms of five years. But Mugabe insisted that his two terms should begin afresh, allowing him to rule until 2010, or for thirty years in all.

But when the referendum votes were counted, well over half were against the constitution, marking ZANU-PF's first defeat at the polls. A general election was only months away, and if the voting patterns persisted, the party would lose power to the newly formed MDC, led by former trade union boss Morgan Tsvangirai.

Mugabe moved quickly. Within days of the referendum he had harnessed the power of his former guerrillas, most of whom now lived in poverty around the country. Bands of 'war veterans' took charge of the rural areas, and the police were ordered not to intervene when the fighters beat up anyone who could not produce a ZANU-PF membership card.

At the same time the guerrillas started occupying white-owned farms, and, despite losing the referendum, Mugabe rushed through legislation allowing the government to take over any property without payment. He promised to redistribute the land among the black population in return for their votes.

The June 2000 election was marked by violence and intimidation, as veterans, the army, police and the CIO turned on MDC supporters. Even so, the new party won 57 of the 120 contested seats. Under the 1987 changes, Mugabe had granted himself the power to appoint 30 MPs of his own choice, creating a 150-seat parliament and virtually guaranteeing his hold on government.

The next election was a presidential poll in 2002, which saw Mugabe and Tsvangirai squaring off for the top job. By that time the state had set up a youth militia, and rural areas became virtual no-go zones for the opposition.

Stories of rape and torture in the militia camps were recorded by journalists and human rights groups both inside Zimbabwe and working among refugees and exiles in Britain and South Africa. People found in possession of MDC membership cards – or without one for ZANU-PF – were routinely dragged to camps and abused, but the militia told stories of how they themselves were also beaten and often raped as part of their training.

Mugabe won by 1 685 212 votes to Tsvangirai's 1 258 401, giving the president a margin of more than 400 000, but Western observers and a Commonwealth team led by former Nigerian military ruler General Abdusalam Abubakar reported that the elections had been rigged and that intimidation was so rife as to make it impossible to validate the result. The European Union and the United States refused to recognise Mugabe's mandate, and Zimbabwe was suspended from the Commonwealth.

By this time the majority of white farmers had been forced off their land, and, as had been the case with earlier attempts at redistribution, the best farms were handed out to ministers and loyal supporters who helped to keep ZANU-PF in power. When the courts declared the land seizures illegal and upheld claims by black Zimbabweans of torture and abuse, Mugabe forced the judges to resign and appointed his supporters to the bench, turning the judiciary into a rubber stamp.

His idea of settling young people on the land proved unworkable. Having learnt to do algebra and quote Shakespeare, they were not willing to become subsistence farmers, and stayed in town.

By 2004, all but 300 of the original 4 000 white farmers were off the land. One in three black Zimbabweans had left the country, pushed out by violence and inflation running at more than 500 per cent. Cash crops like tobacco, cotton, flowers, corn and vegetables had been among the country's chief exports, earning valuable foreign exchange, but as the sector imploded the economy collapsed and unemployment soared.

Basic foodstuffs, including maize, meat, milk and bread, grew scarce, and, as prices rocketed, the government imposed controls, which, in turn, gave rise to a black market that pushed the cost of goods even higher.

How far Zimbabwe had descended into the abyss was borne out by author Cathy Buckle, whose books *African Tears* and *Beyond Tears* told of the horrors she and other farmers endured during the land campaign. Cathy now lives in the small town of Marondera east of Harare, and every week, through an e-mail newsletter, thousands of people read her sad, though often witty account of daily life in a country gone mad.

Late in 2004, she compiled these statistics:[6]

Year	1999/2000	2003/2004
Cost of 20 cigarettes	Z$22	Z$4 500
Wheat production	314 000 tons	50 000 tons
Cost of one loaf of bread	Z$21	Z$3 500
Milk production	160 000 tons	100 000 tons
Cost of one litre of milk	Z$15	Z$2 600
Cost of one dozen eggs	Z$36	Z$7 500
Cost of one bag of sugar	Z$40	Z$5 303
Tourism earnings	$200 million	$44 million

Cathy ended with a note on the 2004 Harare Agricultural Show, which took place in August. Every year since 1895, farmers have brought their best livestock to town, competing for prizes in the show ring. Great herds of cattle and goats descend on the capital, along with sheep, chickens and other animals. In 2004, the total exhibits were nine cattle, two goats and three sheep.[7]

As the economy collapsed, millions fled the country. Doctors and nurses found employment abroad, and by the end of the first quarter in 2004, the state health system had imploded. Official statistics put the country's AIDS-related deaths at 3 000 a week, and the situation grew steadily worse as people infected with HIV moved rapidly to full-blown AIDS because of poor care and nutrition.

Sexual abuse in the militia camps exacerbated the problem. Rape of both men and women prisoners was widely reported, and militia members – especially young women – were frequently violated. Condoms were rarely available.

Contracting HIV is always a risk in places of detention. In any given year in the United States, for example, nearly 12 million people pass through the prison system, including 17 per cent of all Americans with AIDS. Faced with budget crises, many correctional facilities back away from testing inmates, fearing they will be required to pay for expensive treatments.

Condoms are banned or simply unavailable in nine out of ten US jails, where inmates are vulnerable to AIDS or other blood-borne diseases that are easily spread through male rape or unprotected sex.[8] But in Zimbabwe, the incidence of HIV was as high as 40 per cent in the eighteen to thirty age group, whose members filled the militia camps.

In January 2004, I interviewed a man in Johannesburg who was close to death. Bongani Moyo, aged twenty-five, stood more than two metres in his worn-out tennis shoes, but his legs were thin and the pockets of fat below his eyes had withered, pushing the sockets back and giving his head a skull-like appearance.

Before escaping from a camp near Bulawayo, his job had been to rape women detained for no other reason than supporting the MDC.

'We would be sent out into the countryside to punish people who support the opposition,' he told me. 'We would beat people and sometimes burn down their homes. Other times we were ordered to rape women who did not support the ruling party. If a militia member refused to do this, he himself would be raped, and I saw this happen to other men.'

Bongani's nightmare began in the middle of 2002, when he entered a training camp near Mount Darwin, ninety-six kilometres north-east of Harare, with the promise of a job.

> I had been unemployed for a long time, and I believed that at least I would get some food. But it was worse than anything in my life. There were few meals, we were woken before sunrise and made to run maybe fourteen kilometres [8.5 miles] through the bush, and we were beaten nearly every day. The commanders and trainers used a lot of *mbanje* [marijuana], and forced us also to smoke it.
>
> Then I was deployed to a rural area near Bulawayo, and that is when I died as a human. I had finished my training,

> but I had nowhere to go. I was promoted to a group leader, so at least I got some extra food.
>
> Every day I would wake up and go out like a machine to beat up those who were said to have attended opposition rallies. We even beat mothers whose children had been seen at MDC meetings. I was living in hell twenty-four hours a day, but I had no feeling left for anything, not even for myself.
>
> Then my job changed. I was told to stay at the camp, and when women were brought in accused of making trouble for the ruling party, it was my job to rape them. I don't know how many I raped before I had the courage to escape. But now I am weak and find it hard to breathe. I think God is punishing me with this disease because I did not resist those things.[9]

In 2004, a BBC television news crew interviewed close on a hundred women who had formerly been held in the camps. Half of them claimed they had been raped, including an eleven-year-old girl.

In Harare, the state-owned *Herald* newspaper denounced the BBC, as well as reports criticising the youth training programme, as 'a glaring fiction' compiled by journalists 'plagued with ignorance and malice'. The camps, it said, 'have no ounce of tuition on torture or killing'.

But an official with the ministry of youth, gender and employment creation, which oversees the training, told the BBC: 'You are moulding someone to listen to you. If it means that rape has to take place for that person to take instructions from you, then it's okay.'[10]

Despite huge numbers of former militia pouring into South Africa, Zimbabwe's youth minister, Elliot Manyika, said on state-owned television that there was no truth to stories that recruits were fleeing the camps. 'We can account for 99 per cent of our graduates,' he said.

A twenty-one-year-old former recruit who had escaped to Johannesburg countered the minister's claim in a statement to the media. 'The minister is lying,' he said bluntly. 'There is no food, only pain and suffering, and hundreds are running away. We see them arriving in Hillbrow every day. All are hungry – I would say starving – and many have got injuries where they have been beaten by the camp commanders. Some of the women are pregnant because they were raped for not following orders.'

At the same media conference I met Charlie Dube, who looked eighteen but said he was twenty-five. 'They hated people like me who had finished high school, and they went out of their way to humiliate us,' he said. He was beaten regularly, forced to masturbate in front of his commanders and told that he needed to be re-educated in the ways of ZANU-PF.

He said his group was taught that anyone opposing President Mugabe 'could not be classed as human', and could be beaten or tortured, or even killed; to destroy them was a service to all Zimbabweans. 'Most of the Green Bombers [militia] who leave the camps end up hating ZANU-PF for what has happened to them,' said Charlie. 'Now, with so many running away, we can hope that things will soon change.'

But, despite all the violence, conditions in Zimbabwe, even at the height of Mugabe's rule, were not the worst in Africa, past or present. In the mid-1970s, Ugandan president Idi Amin murdered more than 300 000 of his citizens, with barely a whisper from other African states or the leaders of the free world.

Burundi and Rwanda saw repeated massacres after independence from Belgium in 1962, the most recent being the Rwandan genocide of 1994, when more than 800 000 of the minority Tutsi tribe were slaughtered by the majority Hutus. Again the world did not intervene, and France even assisted the killers with aeroplane loads of weapons flown nightly from Paris to the Rwandan capital of Kigali.[11]

Nigeria suffered a string of coups after independence in 1960, and in 1967, when the province of Biafra tried to break away, more than a million of its people from the Ibo tribe were killed fighting the central government in Lagos, or were systematically starved to death.[12]

In 2003, the government of Sudan armed a state-backed militia known as the Janjaweed, which, by August of that year, had killed an estimated 50 000 black Sudanese in the west of the country and driven more than a million people from their homes.

But what drew global attention to Mugabe's tyranny was his attack on white farmers. If these landowners had been black, it is doubtful that the same level of protest would have been raised when they were forced from their homes. And with so much media attention, it was perhaps inevitable that the image of Robert Mugabe – shaking his fist during a speech to the party faithful and insulting by name the leaders in Europe and America who dared to criticise his policies – became one with Zimbabwe.

Like Hitler's Germany, Stalin's Russia, Castro's Cuba or Saddam Hussein and Iraq, Mugabe's name became shorthand for all that was wrong with the country he ruled, as though he had personally committed every bad deed, every act of mischief. And from that mindset, it was a short hop to the notion that if only the world could get rid of Mugabe, things would come right. Food would appear as if by magic, the exiles would flock home and there would be dancing in the streets.

Perhaps it is for this reason that so little work has been done to plan for change.

A month after the Midrand protest, the demonstrators who had disrupted Dr Gono's meeting reconvened outside the Zimbabwe embassy in Pretoria, and this time there was no hiding their intent. Hundreds of young black men and women waved placards supporting Morgan Tsvangirai or demanding that Mugabe be tried for crimes against humanity. As was their right, they asked their country's most senior diplomat to accept a memorandum of complaint against the government in Harare. Instead, Moyo sent a security guard to receive the letter, and the crowd grew louder, accusing him of cowardice.

If this demonstration had taken place in Zimbabwe, the police would have arrived within minutes and tear-gassed the mob, after which they would have given chase to fleeing protesters, rounding them up to be interrogated later in the cells. But in democratic South Africa, the authorities had sent a single police car to observe the event, and had even granted a permit for the march.

Hard to believe that, just fifteen years earlier, South Africa itself had been under the heel of a government that brooked no protest. The National Party, which invented apartheid and oppressed the nation for almost half a century, lost power in the country's first democratic elections in 1994, and ten years later, in August 2004, it was dissolved, unable to win even 2 per cent of the popular vote.

In Zambia and Malawi and across Africa, the story was often the same. When parties that had dominated the scene for decades lost office, they slipped into obscurity and rarely, if ever, returned to power. The success of South Africa's transformation may well have been on the minds of Zimbabwean protesters as they danced outside the art deco legation in Pretoria's embassy belt on that winter's day in 2004.

The fate of ZANU-PF in a democratic Zimbabwe was just as likely to have been haunting Ambassador Moyo and the president he served.

2

Back to Basics

If we want to climb out of the hole we are in, it is a job for all the people. – Chinua Achebe

FOR AS LONG AS I CAN REMEMBER, THERE HAS BEEN an odd notion in Zimbabwe. When things are bad, people shake their heads and say, 'It's got to get worse before it gets better!' or 'We need to hit the bottom before we start going up.'

Anyone who has spent a few days in the country will have heard these phrases, but the premise that a situation will change once it has reached the base of some imaginary curve defies reason.

In Burma, Sudan, North Korea and other chambers of tyranny, the quality of life has slipped below the general definition of misery and stayed there for years. Just because conditions are as bad as they can be doesn't mean they have to improve ... unless someone or something forces the nation and its leaders to change course.

So, what changes will a new government have to make in Zimbabwe? In 2004, the opposition MDC prepared a comprehensive document called *RESTART*, which outlined key areas that would need attention, including health, education, farming, exports and the attraction of foreign capital, along with plans to develop a true democracy.

The plan was bold and well thought-out, but made no provision for any effort ahead of change to train people or set up structures that could be used to implement the programme. It is just possible that neither the MDC nor ZANU-PF is aware of how badly Zimbabwe's institutions have been eroded.

At a physical level, massive refurbishment will be needed classroom by classroom, clinic by clinic, ward by ward. The list will include radios for police on patrol, vehicles for government departments, blackboards for schools, beds for hospitals, accountability and a transparent tender system.

Get it right, and the money will follow. Donor nations are so used to seeing their cash being wasted that if they can be shown a clear agenda with inventories of what is required and a simple plan for implementation, the money should not be a problem.

Instead, though, we too often see new governments slipping into old ways: fleets of luxury cars for those in charge, grand plans that are big on budget and short on detail, seminars where ministers and their lackeys talk about what needs to be done before they've consulted the people to see what works on the ground.

If you can get the basics right, the grand design will follow. The first question, then, is: How bad are the basics?

In June 2004, Jan Raath, one of the few independent journalists still reporting from Zimbabwe for foreign newspapers,[1] visited a school in Chegutu, 100 kilometres west of Harare. In a story for the London *Times*, he wrote:

> There are no books, no chalk and little hope as children are forced out of class.
>
> Four teachers start each day by washing goat droppings from their primary school's concrete floor. They have no textbooks, no stationery and no chalk; marks on a blackboard show where a teacher has tried to write with charcoal.
>
> There are benches and tables for only ten children: the

> rest are told to bring sacks for seating. In the winter, a cold wind sweeps through the broken windows.
>
> Three quarters of the 176 pupils have been sent home until their parents can pay the 50p term fees.
>
> The school has no money. 'Without the fees, we can do nothing,' said the headmaster, who asked not to be named. A teacher added: 'We ask the children to give us their chewing gum so we can stick pictures on the wall.'
>
> As recently as 2000, primary school enrolment was 93 per cent, the highest in Africa. But the figure had slumped to 65 per cent by last year [2003], according to Unicef. Literacy among schoolchildren, once 86 per cent, is plummeting and dropout rates are soaring. In addition, the land seizures have forced 121 000 children of commercial farm workers out of school.
>
> 'If the current situation continues, we will lose a whole generation,' Cecile Baldeh, Unicef's project officer in Zimbabwe, said.

At the same time as Raath wrote his story, President Mugabe awarded himself a 2 500 per cent pay increase, yet the government was unable to maintain school buildings in urban or rural areas and could barely pay its 109 000 teachers. In Harare, Raath visited what used to be one of the city's better state schools.

> Cranborne High, in a middle-class area of Harare, was built in the 1960s, with a large assembly hall, fully equipped gymnasium, competition-standard swimming pool and an art and design centre.
>
> Today it is desolate, reeking of urine. The pool is a yard deep in algae, the rugby posts are buckled and all the gym equipment has been stolen. In the woodwork rooms, only the vices remain, bolted to the tables. The hall is coated in dust and grime. Classroom windows have been smashed and doors torn off their hinges.[2]

But there was money available for other priorities. In August 2004, Mugabe spent Z$18 billion ($1.8 million) on new cars for his generals, brigadiers and air chiefs. Army spokesperson Lieutenant Colonel Ben Ncube said he found nothing unusual about the purchase. 'Do you expect to see guys like brigadiers moving around in Mazda 323s?' he asked one reporter who questioned the deal. 'They are senior people and they deserve cars like that.'[3]

In the townships around the capital, anything up to 20 per cent of primary school children are orphans, and more than half have only one parent. There are hundreds of thousands of orphan families in Zimbabwe, headed by the eldest of the surviving children, and, as inflation drives up school fees, more of them – and even lucky youngsters with one or both parents alive – will drop out after only a year or two of high school.

Tapson Moyo is eighteen, and with both parents dead from AIDS, he looks after his fourteen-year-old sister Beauty and eight-year-old brother Albert. The three live in a single room in Seke township south of Harare, and Tapson spends the day buying and selling stationery, and delivering paper, pens, staples and other office supplies to secretaries and businesses in the CBD.

His mark-up is 30 per cent, and with this and some money sent to him every month by a white Zimbabwean woman who once employed his mother and now lives in the UK, he pays school fees for his siblings and keeps them in food and clothes.

Three nights a week he goes to a small private college to study maths and English. 'I need those two subjects, then I am going to try coaching younger children from wealthy families who are struggling to pass exams,' he said, when we spoke in late 2004. 'I don't know why, but I have a natural talent for maths and my Mum always spoke English to me, so I do well at the language. Maybe I can be a journalist one day.'

Male children have an advantage in a culture that places a higher value on educating the boy child. Young men can work as car guards or even beg on the streets, but they chase away women who try to compete.

Girls who have not completed their education can work as housemaids or cleaners, but with so many of the wealthier class now living abroad, jobs are few. And then there's the old fallback: in a country where prostitution is a crime, a secret army comes out at night to work the pavements in Harare, Bulawayo and Victoria Falls. Among their ranks are under-age girls working for bread and school fees.

Like their students, teachers also have it rough, though for different reasons. Daniel Madziwa is a primary school teacher whose family hails from the Chinhoyi region, 100 kilometres north of Harare. After graduating from training college, he joined the ministry of education and was posted to a rural school in the Midlands province, south of the capital.

Now living in South Africa, he told me about the problems that have seen thousands of teachers leave the country.

> I loved my work, I mean really loved it. Teaching was all I had wanted to do since my teenage years, and I had been posted to a good school with a headmaster who worked hard to achieve results.
>
> But the government kept raising school fees and I saw many kids dropping out because their parents couldn't afford it, and I even coached some of them after hours without charge.
>
> Then in 2002 a group of war veterans and youth militia came to the school and accused the headmaster of supporting the MDC. They said he had been seen at an opposition rally, and they lined up the teachers and the children and forced us to watch while they stripped him naked and beat him with rubber pipes and lengths of copper wire.

> Kids were crying, but there was nothing anyone could do because there were so many of the veterans and Bombers.
>
> The war vets then told all the support staff, including gardeners and cleaners, that they were fired, and veterans took over the work instead. Every teacher was required to join ZANU-PF and to have a party card on hand at any time. The new gardeners and cleaners became our bosses, and they were often drunk and would come into class shouting abuse at the teacher and ordering the children into the playground for political stuff.
>
> When school closed for the Christmas holidays at the end of 2003, I took a bus to South Africa. I have no papers here, so I now work as a part-time cleaner, but I could not continue teaching under those conditions.

Even Amnesty International (AI) complained to the Zimbabwe government over what it described as the widespread 'persecution, harassment and torture of students and teachers'. This followed a strike by teachers' organisations with support from the Zimbabwe National Students' Union. Police rounded up leaders of both groups and tortured them with electric shocks.

In a letter to the Minister for Home Affairs (who was also responsible for police), AI pointed out that 'torture and cruel, inhuman or degrading treatment or punishment are forbidden according to Article 5 of the African Charter on Human and People's Rights to which Zimbabwe is party'.[4]

But the repression continued.

In its *RESTART* paper, the MDC pledged to rebuild the education system, and recognised quality education as a right. And it laid out the following key steps:[5]

Preschool	Primary school	Secondary school
Ensure that all preschools are registered	Make the first seven years of school compulsory, with state support for those in need	Ensure that all students have access to secondary education, especially girls
Aim for all children to attend at least one year of kindergarten	Structure primary education as preparation for high school	Professionalise school committees, boards and associations
Allocate resources to the sector	Focus on foundation subjects, including language, maths, science and AIDS awareness	Continually upgrade teacher competence
	Expand the teaching of local languages	Add more career subjects to the syllabus
	Improve resources	
	Improve teacher training	

Worryingly, the document also calls for 'religious and moral education'. The ZANU-PF government brands the youth brigade programme a form of moral training, and in a country with diverse religions, the state might be better served by keeping church, mosque, temple and synagogue out of the classroom.

Most disturbingly, *RESTART* gives no hint on *how* a new government would rebuild education. The problems of teachers in exile, AIDS, orphans and a lack of capacity will not be solved with good intentions, or even through funding.

In 1980, Mugabe sent out a worldwide SOS for teachers to help expand his education programme, and received an overwhelming response from Australia and Britain. It was a good idea and could be used again, with donor countries paying the salaries and relocation fees of their own nationals who want to work in Zimbabwe.

In Britain there would probably be a queue as teachers vie for the chance to educate pupils keen to learn. A 2004 report by Cambridge University's education faculty painted a dismal picture of aggressive children, hostile parents and a dumbed-down curriculum in Britain's state schools. As one teacher observed: 'No one else would go to work, be told to "fuck off" and be expected to put up with it.'

Not surprisingly, an increasing amount of school time was being taken up by dealing with misbehaviour, according to the report. Instead of giving lessons, British teachers said, they spent their time writing lengthy reports on pupils who failed to submit homework, disrupted lessons, abused staff, fought with peers and damaged school property.[6]

By contrast, despite the lack of money and resources, schoolchildren in Zimbabwe are respectful, punctual and grateful for whatever education they can get.

This makes the collapse of their schools all the more tragic, but at least in rebuilding the system, a new government could bank on the cooperation and assistance of the people they would be trying most to help.

But there's another problem, one that few people talk about. Figures published by Unicef suggest that 25 per cent of Zimbabwean teachers are HIV-positive, and that by 2010 some 38 000, or just over a third of the current staff, will have died. Given how the disease affects the human body, it is likely they will have left the classroom – weak and short of breath – a year or more before the end. And unless billions have been spent on the country's health system, there will be little help for patients afflicted with a headache, let alone HIV/AIDS.

By 2004, average life expectancy, which stood at fifty-six years in 1975, had slipped to just thirty-three, the lowest in the world. A quarter of the adult population was HIV-positive or suffering from full-blown AIDS, 70 per cent lived below the poverty line, with almost as many not having enough to eat, and the state allocated just 3 per cent of its budget to health, while more than twice that figure was spent on defence.

In 2004, the government bought army vehicles and jet fighters from China for $200 million, while in some rural clinics nurses didn't even have soap to wash their hands.

In the face of wholesale emigration by doctors and nurses and a lack of funds for basic care, the *British Medical Journal* had ranked Zimbabwe as having the worst health system in the world as far back as August 2001, placing it at the bottom of a World Health Organisation list of 191 nations. And AIDS is not the only problem.

Urban accommodation in Zimbabwe has not kept pace with the massive shift of people from rural areas. As a result, there is overcrowding in all the dormitory towns around Harare, Bulawayo and Mutare, and even smaller centres like Gweru and Masvingo. This has seen an increase in TB, asthma and other respiratory diseases.

Water treatment has suffered because foreign currency is not always available to import chlorine and other chemicals, and gastro-intestinal diseases are common. Outbreaks of cholera and typhoid are annual events; waste disposal is erratic, and when people get sick, they are hard-pressed to find help.

On average, developed countries have 320 doctors per 100 000 people. In Africa, it's only twelve,[7] and Zimbabwe falls near the bottom of that list, with just six.[8] Even Afghanistan is higher at eleven.

And Zimbabwe's medical statistics may be worse than they appear, because many doctors leaving the country do not seek to have their names removed from professional registers. Out of 1 200 physicians trained in Zimbabwe in the 1990s, 840 had emigrated by the end of that decade. By 2005, some specialists were down to single digits, while in rural areas the government introduced ox-drawn ambulances because fuel and spare parts couldn't be found for the vehicles that used to transport patients to hospital.

The cost of seeing a private doctor was more than the average monthly wage.

Somewhere in the order of 40 000 Zimbabwean nurses work outside the country, and persuading them – and thousands of doctors – to come home would be a near-impossible task. And the problem is not exclusive to Zimbabwe. Botswana, Africa's best-governed country, is struggling to keep its medical staff, who are tempted by higher wages overseas.

More than 21 000 Nigerian doctors work in the United States. In Francophone Africa, the problem is even more acute, with medical staff moving to Belgium, France and Canada. More Benin-trained doctors work in France than in their own country.

It costs $60 000 to train a doctor in the developing world, and $12 000 for a nurse. Using these figures, poor countries lose about $500 million every year in medical migration to the West.

In 2004, health minister David Parirenyatwa said people who chose to leave the country were unpatriotic, and announced that locally trained doctors and nurses would, in future, be bonded to the state for the same number of years as it took them to qualify. But the president of the nurses' association, Clara Nondo, scoffed at the measures. 'The government needs to address the primary causes why professionals in the health sector are trooping out of the country,' she told a newspaper. 'Bonding will not stop the brain drain because it's about bread and butter issues, not patriotism.'[9]

Dr Andrea Tasker is an American who did volunteer work in Zimbabwe from April to July 2004. Her impressions summed up the problems faced by doctors trying to keep the health system afloat.

I worked as a volunteer physician at a hospital eighty kilometres north of Harare, and what I witnessed there was horrific: a mix of the AIDS pandemic and an intense political/economic crisis.

The medical infrastructure in Zimbabwe is limited to begin with. Add to that a situation in which one in three adults have HIV (and no access to antiretrovirals) and the result, at the ground zero level, is unimaginable human suffering. Patients with medical complications of HIV are packed into run-down wards. The morgues are full to capacity and the coffin industry is booming.

My hospital had only two or three permanent doctors serving an immediate population of 100 000 people and acting as a referral hospital for a further 250 000.

I went there to practice my specialty, obstetrics and gynaecology, but out of necessity did everything from paediatrics to emergency medicine.

Nights on call for me were a mixture of performing emergency C sections and admitting weak, anaemic, emaciated, febrile, coughing HIV patients to administer IV antibiotics and analgesia. There was only one oxygen tank for the whole hospital, and sometimes that was empty.

The workload for the doctors in Zimbabwe is overwhelming. These are trained professionals with excellent medical skills who receive the equivalent of $50 a week in a country plagued by hyperinflation.

Phone lines are unreliable; radio and TV are little more than propaganda; and there is a fuel crisis, making travel difficult. It is isolation in the truest sense of the word.

And some months, doctors are not paid at all because the state has no funds. One GP was recently able to access only one per cent of his monthly salary or $2.10.

Zimbabwe will need freedom and a new economic structure before the health system can be fixed. An inventory of hospitals and clinics will show what drugs and equipment are needed, and donor countries are sure to help fund the programme. The MDC has made the usual calls of a party in opposition, and says that among its first actions in office will be to tackle malnutrition, immunisation, and HIV and associated trauma, while also improving access to safe drinking water and essential drugs.

The new government will set up a National Health Board to coordinate input from all stakeholders, and the Treasury will comply with African Union, Southern African Development Community (SADC) and United Nations standards that call for at least 15 per cent of the national budget to be spent on health.

Rhodesia and Zimbabwe (until the early 1990s) had a good district health system, with virtually free medical care for anyone who could get to a clinic. The MDC has committed itself to rebuilding that structure, and will undertake a step-by-step audit of all facilities, from maternity wards to mortuaries, while also tackling the basic issues of water, sanitation, research and disease control.

The party's written proposals on health are impressive, but, again, no attention is paid to the *how*. Getting skills back into the country will be difficult, but a start could be made by setting up Zimbabwe medical associations in Britain, the US and South Africa, where a large number of doctors and nurses have settled.

Skilled people in the diaspora – doctors, nurses, teachers, farmers, vets, lawyers, judges, police, media workers, economists and every other trade and profession – have to be harnessed in advance to give credence to the blueprint. If these people can contribute to a plan for the future, there is more chance that, come the change, they will want to continue playing a role in rebuilding the country.

Ndioro Ndiaye, a native of Senegal, is deputy director-general of the Geneva-based International Organisation for Migration. She believes that qualified people in various sectors may be tempted to support the reconstruction programme, provided they do not have to sacrifice what they have built up in their new countries.

When I asked her about the brain drain, she said there was a chance that skilled people could be tempted back to their former homes, but only if governments proved flexible and open-minded. 'If health professionals are not required to choose between two lifestyles,' she said, 'and if they are guaranteed freedom of movement as well as fair remuneration and special arrangements with their employers, whether public or private, they may return to do short spells of work.'

In West Africa, thousands of people come and go, working at home for anything from a few weeks to several months, then returning to their new countries, where they earn hard currency.

But without political change it would be hard to lure people back to Zimbabwe, where the educated ranks, including teachers and medical staff, are often branded as 'enemies of the state' because they question the collapse going on around them. In cases where schools have been trashed or clinics raided by war veterans or the youth brigade, the police have too often been unwilling to intervene for fear of upsetting the government that pays them.

Without the rule of law, little can be achieved, and until that problem is fixed, the old saying is probably accurate: things *are* going to get worse before they get better.

3

Law of the Land

One has a moral responsibility to disobey unjust laws.
– Martin Luther King

IT WAS PAST MIDNIGHT AND I WAS LYING ON MY STOMACH at the foot of the bed, striking matches in the dark while the crowd watched at the window, waiting for the monster to show itself.

There was a scratching sound somewhere deep under the bed, but with all the excited talk outside, I couldn't hear much.

'Quiet!' I shouted, and, as if God himself had spoken, the chatter stopped mid-breath as I struck another match. And there she was: a six-foot-something cobra, her shiny coils jet black, hood slightly raised, staring at me from the corner where the bed nuzzled the wall, tongue flicking as she tried to catch my scent.

She? Most black Egyptians (cobras, that is) are female, while the males come in an assortment of browns, greys and even a banded variety.

The room was tiny – maybe two metres by four – with only the bed, a chair, a small wardrobe and no electricity: typical accommodation for the millions who survive below the poverty line in the urban sprawl near Harare, in this case the dormitory town of Budiriro.[1]

Tommy Chipanga, the young man who lived there, had climbed into bed at around 10 p.m., and was dozing off when a movement caught his eye. A rat was sitting on top of his cupboard, cleaning its face and looking down at him. Then, as he stared, Tommy saw the snake lift its head and strike. The rat jumped, the snake caught it in mid-air and, overbalancing, toppled onto the bed, still holding its dinner.

'I pulled the blanket over my head,' Tom told me when I met him at Budiriro police station at around 11.30 p.m. 'But as I lifted the blanket, I heard the snake crashing onto the floor. I jumped up and stood on the bed, but I couldn't see it, so I stepped onto the chair and climbed out of the window and went to call the police.'

Constable Richard Phiri had telephoned me from the charge office, and now here I was with him, standing on the bed as I tried my best to draw the reptile from her lair. For years I have raised funds for the SPCA by rescuing snakes from people's homes at no charge, provided they make a donation to what I regard as one of the world's most worthwhile charities. In the squatter camps and townships there was no fee, and I also conducted free classes on how to recognise the different kinds of snakes.

For some reason many Africans think all snakes are deadly creatures bent on notching up more human victims than Freddy Krueger. In truth, of the 138 species that occupy the subcontinent, only a quarter are lethal, and no more than a dozen could be considered a threat to human life. In Zimbabwe there are probably fewer than six deaths a year from snakebite, and you have more chance of being struck by lightning.[2]

But snakes, along with owls and hyenas, are seen as agents from the dark side, sent by witches to wreak havoc. I caught my first snake when I was ten, and have been fascinated by the reptiles ever since that summer day in Bulawayo nearly forty years ago. With neither legs nor arms, they can swim and climb trees. People evolved perhaps 2 million years ago, but snakes have survived a hundred times longer, thrive in any environment except the polar regions, and will probably be here well after we are gone.

The cobra pressed herself against the wall as I struck another match and manoeuvred the catching stick with my right hand.

'Do you need some help?' asked Constable Phiri, and he held out the cloth bag I had given him when we entered the room. We had been on several missions together, and he always came up trumps; although he was half my age, I admired this young officer who was smart and courteous and never flinched from duty.

'I could use a torch. Surely someone must have a light?'

A cry went out through the crowd. 'Torch! Torch! Mr Snake needs a torch!'

By now I had clasped the terrified cobra in the end of my stick, a device designed for paraplegics with a handle at one end that, when pressed, closed a pair of foam-lined jaws at the other. It had caught her mid-body, which left a metre of the business end swaying, hood like a spinnaker. Egyptians don't spit, but I was wearing goggles anyway, standard equipment when you don't know what kind of snake you're after.

'No one has a torch,' said Richard, still perched on the bed but stepping back against the wall as the snake appeared. I stood up and held the stick down on the floor. At two metres long it kept the lady a safe distance from my legs, but she was frantic now, and with a gulp she regurgitated the rat, which lay glistening in a shroud of slime and stomach acid.

'Okay, give me the bag.' Richard handed me the sack. I looked around the room and saw a broom, propped up against the wall near the bed.

'Take the broom and gently press the brush end down on

her head.' He did as I asked, and I placed my boot on her neck. 'Okay, you can lift the broom.'

Gently, I moved my foot to the last vertebrae, then handed the snake stick to the policeman, who held the trigger while I took her head in my hand, holding her jaws closed as I slipped her into the bag. In her lower coils were the telltale lumps of pregnancy, half-formed eggs the size of new potatoes, pressing their shape through the skin.

I held the bag aloft, and the crowd at the door cheered. I don't think those at the window could see much through the dark, but they took up the sound, and, as Richard Phiri and I walked out, the crowd parted, clapping, whistling, jumping and patting my colleague in congratulation, but never touching me. Some, no doubt, thought I had magic powers, and the rest were taking no chances.

Over the years I had come to know many of the police around Harare. Sometimes they phoned me for help or, if their lines were down, they would arrive at my home, day or night, and together we would set out to collect a snake.

Often, people told tales of huge serpents, always black mambas – Africa's deadliest reptile – but more often than not I came home with a small house snake or some other harmless creature.

Once, a sergeant phoned me from Ruwa, thirty kilometres west of the capital, to say there was a small snake living in the outside toilet behind the charge office. It turned out to be a twelve-foot python, and when I asked him why he had lied, he smiled coyly and said, 'I didn't think you would come if you knew how big it was.'

I never keep wild animals in captivity, so all my catches were released on a private game reserve a thirty-minute drive from town. Sadly, that land was invaded in 2002 by war veterans and all the game was killed, but hopefully the snakes survived.

Zimbabwe's police force dates back to 1899, a year before the Pioneer Column raised the Union Jack in Salisbury. As part of his plan to occupy Matabeleland and Mashonaland, Cecil John Rhodes set up a military unit, the British South Africa Company Police, later abbreviated to BSAP.

In a fairly short time the force had a majority of black members, but in Rhodesia only white recruits could gain a commission, while blacks, no matter how talented or how many years they served in the force, could rise no higher than sergeant major. Things changed in 1978, and after Mugabe took office there was rapid promotion of black officers in the renamed Zimbabwe Republic Police, or ZRP, while some former guerrillas from ZANLA and ZIPRA were pushed into the force without proper training.

A shortage of vehicles and equipment led to a massive rise in crime, but the ZRP remained a fine force, and as recently as 2000, officers in charge of police stations would drill their men and women daily and maintain extensive logs and wall charts tracking the number of crimes in their zone, and the rate at which these were solved.

The police remained a courteous and professional organisation, but while members of the government lavished money on themselves with posh cars and trips abroad, the public service was in a dire state. At every police station from Harare Central to small country towns, buildings were in need of paint; tarred driveways, laid before 1980, were cracked and peeling; pens and stationery ran out with crippling frequency and no one, it seemed, was issued with a torch.

Yet there was always money for riot gear, automatic weapons and tear gas to arm a force that, until 1995, did not even carry handguns.

Despite the best efforts of good people like Richard Phiri, basic policing and crime investigation collapsed, and a once-proud force was turned into just another arm of ZANU-PF, tasked not with keeping the nation safe, but keeping the party in power.

When the land invasions started in 2000, the police reacted instinctively and arrested the war veterans, until being ordered not to do so by Commissioner Augustine Chihuri, a close ally of Mugabe. And when the MDC looked like winning the next election, ruling party thugs were allowed to beat and torture members of the opposition while the police stood by.

Although Chihuri promised that officers would provide 'fair policing to various political persuasions', he also made it clear that 'not supporting the government of the day is tantamount to rebellion, which is a punishable offence'.

By May 2004, the situation had become so serious that Amnesty International issued a warning. 'Repressive legislation and partisan policing are combining to seriously undermine basic rights in Zimbabwe,' the organisation said in a statement. 'Law enforcement officers, who should safeguard the rights of all Zimbabweans, are instead placing those rights under siege.'[3]

The evidence presented by AI and other human rights groups was damning, and fell into four categories:

- Violence perpetrated for the most part by government supporters while police stood by and refused to intervene.
- A refusal to investigate such violence after the fact and to arrest suspected perpetrators.
- Harassment and arrest of opposition members during peaceful demonstrations or when they tried to defend themselves against attacks by ZANU-PF-led groups.
- Human rights violations committed by police officers themselves.

There is no exact tally of the number of people who were harassed, assaulted and tortured in Zimbabwe between 2000 and 2005, but it could exceed half a million. The collected case histories prepared by human rights groups run to thousands of pages, but the following examples will illustrate the extent to which the police had become part of the problem.

2001: Research by Radio Netherlands estimated that more than 40 000 people were tortured and abused during the year,[4] while AI claimed there were 'forced evictions, arbitrary arrests, beatings, torture and political killings amounting to a pattern of deliberate state-sponsored repression of opposition to government policies'. In many cases, according to AI, 'the police not only stood by and failed to intervene in assaults by war veterans and the militia, but actively took part in a number of attacks alongside ZANU-PF supporters'.[5]

On 7 April, Tawanda Hondora, chairman of Zimbabwe Lawyers for Human Rights, was kicked, whipped and beaten by ZANU-PF supporters at Chikomba, north of Harare, when he visited the area to talk to witnesses in another case of intimidation that was about to go to court. Police watched the attack but took no action, and when Hondora reported the incident to his local station in Harare, the police at Chikomba denied that the attack had ever taken place.

On 8 April, students at the University of Zimbabwe staging a peaceful campus demonstration against a cut in college grants were set upon by police, and twenty-eight were injured. One student, Batanai Hadzidzi, was beaten to death. The next day, Hadzidzi's friends mounted a fresh protest to draw attention to his death, but were dispersed when police opened fire with live ammunition.

In June, Zondiwa Dumukani, a thirty-two-year-old driver working on a farm near Harare airport, was beaten to death by a group of eight war veterans while police watched and failed to intervene. The killers alleged that he had not shown up for a ZANU-PF meeting. When Dumukani's employer, a white farmer, reported the murder to the police, they took no action against the war veterans, but instead arrested the farmer and thirty of his staff 'for assaulting members of the ruling party'.

In August, Douglas Chapotera, MDC deputy chairman for Makoni West, had his house set on fire when fifty ruling party supporters arrived just before midnight, brandishing pick handles. While Chapotera and his wife, niece and four children hid inside, they smashed the doors and windows, then doused the house with petrol and set it ablaze.

The family fled, then realised that their baby son was still in the burning building, and as they tried to fight their way back into the house, the mob beat them so badly that Mrs Chapotera had to be admitted to hospital, where her baby was treated for burns. The incident was reported to the police, but by the end of the year they had neither arrested anyone nor gathered any evidence.

Opposition activist Laban Chiweta died in hospital from burns and head injuries after National Youth Service militia attacked him and others in the town of Trojan Mine near Bindura on 6 December. The attacks were carried out in the presence of police officers, who neither intervened nor arrested the assailants.

2002: In January, police stood by while close on 100 youth militia assaulted and harassed residents in the Harare suburb of Kuwadzana. Similar attacks in the town of Marondera in February went unchallenged by police.

In the run-up to the March presidential election, the police refused to comply with court orders to prevent violent attacks and the forced displacement of thousands of farm workers by government supporters.

Torture by both police and state-sponsored militia was widely reported, and opposition members of parliament were arrested on murder charges based on confessions made under duress.

Journalists were arbitrarily detained. In many cases the police did not take action to prevent or investigate killings of opposition supporters by state-sponsored militia.

The Commonwealth Observer Group found that 'very often, the police did not take action to investigate reported cases of violence and intimidation during the election, especially against known or suspected supporters of the MDC. Indeed, they appeared to be high-handed in dealing with the MDC and lenient towards supporters of ZANU-PF. This failure to impartially enforce the law calls seriously into question the application of the rule of law in Zimbabwe.'[6]

Examples of police action during the election were legion, but two cases stood out. At Muzarabani, north-east of Harare near the Mozambique border, when MDC polling agents arrived on the Friday before voters went to the polls, police stopped their vehicles, confiscated the keys and then watched as the local ZANU-PF member of parliament, Nobbie Dzinzi, and a group of war vets set fire to the cars.

In the same area, a further twenty-seven MDC agents were arrested and their vehicles impounded before they reached their destination.

At polling stations across the country, ballot boxes went missing for hours at a time, and when MDC officials asked for details, they were either chased away by police and militia, or arrested and held in custody until after the election results were announced.

2003: On 29 May, the MDC called for peaceful protest marches from 2 to 6 June. On Monday 2 June, the police and army responded with mass arbitrary arrests and attacks on opposition supporters.

Two people died and more than 400 were arrested across the country. In the Harare suburb of Highfield, protesters were intercepted by the police and army, who fired live ammunition into a crowd, causing several injuries.

More than 150 people wounded in similar attacks were taken to the privately run Avenues Clinic in Harare for treatment. As they waited to see doctors, ten police officers entered the clinic, harassed and threatened their earlier victims and abducted seven patients.[7]

At the University of Zimbabwe, riot police, army officers and 'war veterans' cordoned off a march, firing tear gas and using water cannons on student protesters. Forty-nine students were taken to Parirenyatwa Hospital for treatment.

On Tuesday 3 June, MDC member Tichaona Kaguru and MDC councillor for Mbare, Sydney Mazaranhanga, were beaten by police using whips, rubber batons and sticks. As a result of his injuries, Kaguru died the same day.

2004: In April, members of the National Constitutional Assembly (NCA), a civil society group, were assaulted by police when they attempted to hold a peaceful demonstration in Harare.

On the same day, in Bulawayo, the deputy national chairperson of the Zimbabwe Human Rights Association, Mrs Sheba Phiri, and some NCA activists were arrested and detained at the central police station for several hours before being released without charge.

In Harare on 22 April, MDC activist Tinashe Chimedza, who had been due to speak at a youth forum in Mount Pleasant Hall, was assaulted by police using batons, booted feet and open fists. A lawyer called to the scene was initially refused access to Chimedza, who was then arrested and charged with assaulting a police officer.

At the station, the police verbally abused lawyers representing

Chimedza, and one attorney was briefly detained without charge. Chimedza spent the next week in hospital recovering from his injuries.

On 16 June, forty-three women were arrested while attending a private meeting. Police officers used whips to beat some of them on the soles of their feet before releasing them without charge. On 19 June, more than seventy women were arrested in Bulawayo ahead of a demonstration to mark World Refugee Day.

But there were also cases, over the years, in which the police and their commanders applied the law professionally and fairly, arresting activists from the ruling party who had committed criminal acts. Some of these officers were subsequently transferred or threatened with dismissal.

Two senior assistant commissioners – Solomon Ncube, head of the Criminal Investigation Department, and Emmanuel Chimwanda, the Harare provincial commander – were transferred in October 2000. Along with another estimated twenty officers, they were relegated, without duties, desk or command, to what is known as the 'Commissioner's Pool' at police headquarters, a holding pen for those members suspected of opposition sympathies.

They were replaced by colleagues who demonstrated loyalty to the ruling party by detaining opposition activists on the basis of insufficient evidence, or failing to investigate human rights abuses and other criminal acts by government supporters.

And to help those police who wished to do the party's bidding, parliament passed laws that criminalised what are considered basic rights in a democratic society.

Perhaps the worst of the new bills was the Public Order and Security Act (POSA), which, among other things, made it an offence for two or more people to attend a meeting without police permission. Under Section 16 of POSA, it is an offence to engender feelings of hostility towards the president, and the charge carries a fine of Z$100 000 or five years' imprisonment, or both.[8]

Yet not even POSA went far enough, and police began routinely ignoring the few laws that still protected civilian rights. No person in Zimbabwe may be held without charge for more than forty-eight hours, so detainees are moved from station to station and even to other towns for days – even weeks – on end, without appearing before a magistrate. Lawyers and family of the accused cannot find the person and often don't even know of the arrest.

And once in detention, legal or otherwise, suspects are often tortured, despite the fact that under Zimbabwean law, evidence obtained in this way may not be used in court. But, even so, the practice is widespread.

In 2002, Sazzin Mpofu was arrested on suspicion of murdering Bulawayo war veterans' leader Cain Nkala. Over the next two days police beat Mpofu at Bulawayo police station, hitting him with their fists and whipping the soles of his feet.

'Still I said I knew nothing,' Sazzin told me during an interview in Johannesburg in 2004. He continued:

> Then I was taken to an office in the station and tied to a chair, and when another policeman entered, the ones who had been beating me started to laugh. 'I am Inspector Matira,' the new man said, 'and I will make you talk. You have been brave with these other men, but not now, now you will tell me everything.'
>
> Then he knelt in front of me and pulled down my shorts and underpants. One of his assistants handed him some sort of box which had a handle on one side and wires running from the other. Matira lifted my penis and attached the wires to my testicles, using some kind of metal clips.

He placed the box on a desk and slowly turned the handle and I could feel a mild electric current. 'Don't try to be a big man,' Matira said, and he smiled, and the others laughed again.

Then one man came over and pulled my knees apart and two others held me tight against the chair and Matira wound the handle, slow, then fast, and the pain ran into my stomach, my lungs, into my throat and my brain and I screamed and bit my tongue so hard that blood came into my mouth, but still he kept winding. When he stopped, the pain was so bad I felt as though I had left my body and I was floating somewhere near the ceiling.

Then Matira asked me if I had murdered Cain Nkala, and I nodded. I would have confessed to eating my own children rather than take that pain.

Inspector Martin Matira's name crops up repeatedly in the testimony of torture victims.

Mpofu and three others – Remember Moyo, his brother Gilbert and Ketani Sibanda – were held for more than two years pending trial, and Mpofu spent nine months in solitary confinement. Another accused, Matshobane Ngwenya, escaped to South Africa. But the court dismissed the case, citing poor investigation and rejecting confessions obtained under torture.

A new Zimbabwe will need a new constitution and the abolition of laws like POSA and those that muzzle the press. A bill of rights would also help to open up democratic space so long denied to opposition parties, non-governmental organisations, writers and the general population.

The critics dismiss bills of rights and good constitutions, saying that when you have a good government, you don't need this kind of protection, and when bad people run the country, no piece of paper will stand in their way.

But evil laws are the real stuff of tyranny, and for as long as they remain on the books, government can stand at arm's length from its own acts of oppression, while the police arrest dissenters and charge them with breaking laws that should not be there in the first place.

Throughout history, the law has been put to good use. Through it, human rights have passed into statute, slavery has been abolished and free speech guaranteed to all who do not incite the hatred of others. But too often the same craft has been used to criminalise whole sections of the population:

- Nazi Germany passed special laws (some retrospectively) to rob Jews of their property and banish them to concentration camps.
- Saudi Arabia has legislation that makes women second-class citizens, banning them from such basic activities as driving a car.
- In Africa, under French, British, German, Portuguese, Spanish and Belgian colonial rule, there were laws that discriminated against the black majority and often allowed unelected governors to rule by decree.
- Kenyan president Jomo Kenyatta made it a capital offence to discuss his death or what might happen to the country once he left office.
- The majority of African nations have, at various times, been one-party states with laws that banned all political activity except by the ruling clique.
- Ghana's first president, Kwame Nkrumah, placed himself above the courts, with the power to set aside any verdict that displeased him.
- When the white South African government divided the nation into its various colours and tribes, laws were passed to cover every last act of apartheid. For example, it was illegal for people from two different races to have sex with one another.

- Further back in history, some European countries made it fair game to burn witches, castrate lunatics and torture anyone not deemed to be following the word of God.

Just because something is legal, that doesn't make it right.

Among the SADC countries – with the exception of South Africa (and that only since 1994) – the Zimbabwe government's use of both the law and the police as tools of oppression does not stand out as anything special. Arbitrary arrest and illegal detention are common throughout the region, and while interrogating suspects, police will steer them towards a confession simply in order to conclude their investigation, and often resort to torture. Compounding the problem is the weakness of police procedures, including proper record-keeping, to guard against these abuses.

Police in Angola demand cash from street vendors and prostitutes, and beat them if they do not comply. During the second civil war, from 1992 to 2002, the government deployed the PIR (Rapid Intervention Squad), which carried out thousands of extra-judicial executions of people suspected of supporting the opposition UNITA party led by the late Jonas Savimbi.

Harassing the media is fair sport in Malawi, Namibia, Swaziland and Zambia, where journalists have been subjected to arrest, detention, and search and seizure of notes and files when police have tried to suppress publication of articles critical of the government.

Journalists in Malawi have been arrested on a variety of charges, including sedition and 'publishing false news likely to cause public fear or alarm', and even vendors selling independent publications have been beaten up and their papers destroyed.

In Tanzania, members of opposition groups have been repeatedly arrested, beaten or killed before and during demonstrations.

In October 2000, scores of people were injured when police in Zanzibar fired live ammunition, tear gas and rubber bullets at demonstrators protesting against irregularities in the presidential elections. Other groups were fired on from a police helicopter.

In Swaziland, trade unionists have been subject to police raids, arbitrary arrest, torture and ill treatment, and have suffered severe restrictions on their freedom of expression, assembly and association.

And in Zambia, police have routinely abused their powers under the 1996 Public Order (Amendment) Act to deny the right of assembly to opposition groups and government critics, although ruling party rallies do not seem bound by its requirements.[9]

But there have also been accounts of good law enforcement. In Lesotho, which ratified the Convention Against Torture in 2001, the government established an inter-ministerial committee to oversee its implementation, and plans to translate the convention into Sesotho and to criminalise torture. Namibia has a police ombudsman, who receives more than 200 complaints every year.

In late 1998, the South African Police Service adopted a policy on the prevention of torture and the treatment of people in custody, regulating the detention and interrogation of criminal suspects at police stations, and providing safeguards in areas such as record-keeping and medical care. And the country's Bill of Rights dictates that the state cannot discriminate against anyone on grounds of race, gender, sex, pregnancy, marital status, ethnic or social origin, colour, sexual orientation, age, disability, religion, conscience, belief, culture or language.[10]

But while laws may be altered in a matter of weeks, changing attitudes can take far longer. Central to improving the conduct of police in Zimbabwe – and throughout southern Africa – is the need for training.

The level of instruction at Harare's Morris Depot remains high. New officers are schooled in discipline, drill, law, court procedure, weaponry, riot control, administrative procedure, driving and basic skills required on the beat.

However, scant attention is paid to human rights, and since 2002 all officers have undergone a retraining programme that emphasises loyalty to ZANU-PF and instils in students a loathing for minorities, especially whites. According to one report, clips are taken from old Hollywood movies about the slave trade, showing black people tied to trees and being whipped by their white masters, but the class is told that the images are from Zimbabwe pre-1980 and that this was how black people were treated before Mugabe saved the country from oppression.

A local NGO, the Legal Resources Foundation, conducted human rights training for approximately 1 500 serving police officers from 1989 to 1997, and in 1998 the Human Rights Trust of Southern Africa (SAHRIT) began working with the police to develop course materials, but the initiative was suspended in 2001.

Training programmes for a new police force in a democratic Zimbabwe should be developed ahead of change. When freedom comes, it will be essential to reorientate the force, but this will take time. If new manuals and systems had already been developed, the transformation would be faster, and that could only be good for a new democracy.

One example of the kind of things that need to be taught can be found in the procedures laid down by international and regional human rights groups on how police should handle a complaint against the force. The UN General Assembly has stressed that 'all allegations of torture and other cruel, inhuman or degrading treatment should be promptly and impartially investigated by the competent national authority'.[11] Essential elements of a good investigation would include:

- *promptness* to protect the victim and minimise loss of evidence;
- *impartiality* to ensure that due weight is given to all evidence from complainant, accused and witnesses;
- *independence* to ensure no conflict of interest, concealment of evidence or unfair procedure;
- *protection* to ensure no reprisals;
- *thoroughness* in considering all relevant information for proving or dismissing the complaint.

Police suspected of torture or ill treatment should be suspended from active duty during an official investigation, without prejudice to the outcome.[12] But that assumes a service staffed by competent men and women who know how to conduct an investigation. Instead, political appointments and a high rate of attrition have produced a force thin on skills.

There was a time when the ZRP was considered the best in Africa, solving crimes and catching criminals at a higher rate than many developed countries. And there is no reason why this proud reputation cannot be regained.

Redeveloping capacity in the force will be a slow job and will almost certainly require outside help. And this is one area where there are plenty of resources:

- The International Police Association, of which Zimbabwe is a member, has access to large amounts of training data.
- Retired police officers from Commonwealth countries, including former Zimbabwean policemen now in South Africa and overseas, could be asked to provide suggestions and blueprints for the new force.
- Universities with law enforcement courses could be asked to assist as part of an aid programme.
- The public needs to be surveyed on its attitude towards and expectations of the police.

With the exception of the last item, much of this work could be started without delay, and exile communities could help with opinions on what is needed to remould the force.

But it is not only the police who have been used to oppress the nation. Members of the youth brigades will need extensive counselling in an effort to rechart their value system. Recruits have been taught that rape and torture are acceptable tools in the war against those who dare to challenge the state, and in the process the perpetrators have themselves become victims.

All the former recruits I interviewed showed signs of post-traumatic stress, and told stories of cruelty and humiliation visited upon them by the camp trainers – skills they, in turn, were encouraged to use against the population.

Tragically, the use of militias has become common in African conflicts.

In Liberia, child soldiers as young as ten were forced into service, manning roadblocks and even forming execution squads. In Sierra Leone, teenage gangs chopped off their opponents' hands, and in the Ivory Coast in November 2004, similar groups conducted house searches in the commercial capital, Abidjan, killing anyone perceived to be against the government.

From February 2003, the Sudan government and its allied Arab militias waged a brutal war against a rebel insurgency in Darfur. In interviews with Sudanese refugees, Human Rights Watch researchers documented widespread abuses committed by government forces acting with the Janjaweed militia.[13]

At the time of writing, that conflict remained unresolved, but work had begun in Sierra Leone to rehabilitate former child soldiers and wean them from their violent past.

Perhaps one of the most successful demobilisations in Africa took place in Rwanda. In May 2004, I visited one of the camps where former members of the Interhamwe militia were being debriefed before returning to civilian life.

Armed and spurred on by the former government, the Interhamwe had killed more than 800 000 of their fellow citizens in just 100 days during 1994. When the government was overthrown, thousands of militia members escaped to the Democratic Republic of Congo, but slowly, and in response to state radio broadcasts, they began trickling into camps along Rwanda's border, where they could be taught basic skills and come to terms with the genocide that had robbed these young men of their innocence.

At the end of the course – during which they learnt skills from literacy to crafts and agriculture – the former soldiers were paid a small sum and allowed to return to their families. Many had been regular members of the old Rwandan army and police, some of whom were forced, or chose, to participate in the killings.

After demobilisation, they were encouraged to come up with a business project that would benefit their community. They would present their plans to a committee and were given seed capital to start the enterprise. I spoke with people in these camps, as well as with their teachers and wardens. All had a positive approach to the programme and to healing Rwanda and making sure that such a tragedy never happens again. This model could be adapted to any country where people have been dehumanised by the state, and those who see themselves as future leaders of Zimbabwe would do well to study it.

Psychologists and psychiatrists have written numerous books and papers on this type of programme, and there are case studies dating back to the Hitler Youth (disbanded in 1945), and more recently from East Timor, central America and South Africa. The challenge is to use this knowledge to devise a programme that can be introduced when democratic space opens up in Zimbabwe.

With a new constitution, reform of the police and an end to the militia, it would be possible to build a legal system worthy of a free country, but it is the courts that carry the burden of justice.

From 2000 there were concerted efforts to undermine the judiciary, and many independent-minded judges and magistrates were replaced with ZANU-PF loyalists, while others were intimidated in an effort to secure a particular judgment.

In August 2004, when high court judge Lawrence Kamocha ordered the release of Harare businessman James Makamba, he received a visit from the CIO.

Makamba had been arrested on five charges of allegedly exporting foreign currency and faced a further six counts for the same offence. The former Zimbabwe Broadcasting Corporation announcer and one-time ZANU-PF MP had already spent seven months in jail awaiting trial, and it was rumoured that the motive behind his detention was an alleged affair with President Mugabe's young wife, Grace.

Court officials, who asked not to be named, told *ZimOnline* news service that CIO agents had accused Kamocha of not protecting the interests of the government when he released Makamba. 'The guys visited him in his chambers ten minutes after the judgment was delivered,' one official said. 'They quizzed him on why he had freed Makamba. I understand they are still calling him and threatening him. We all think that the ruling was very judicial, but that's why he is in trouble, anyway.'[14]

Harassing the judiciary is nothing new. When land invasions began in 2000 and the courts declared them illegal, senior judges – including Chief Justice Anthony Gubbay, who had been appointed by Mugabe in 1990 – were intimidated until they resigned and were replaced by people more closely aligned with the party.

But there were those who stood their ground.

In the trial of the six MDC members accused of killing Cain Nkala, Judge Sandra Mungwira castigated the police for their poor evidence and refused to accept confessions made under torture. Throughout the trial Mungwira – who was undergoing chemotherapy for cancer – was threatened, and CIO agents hounded her clerk, who was asked to snoop on the judge's computer.

Edith Mushore, one of the defence lawyers, was phoned repeatedly after midnight by war veteran Joseph Chinotimba, who had led some of the land invasions and had used the same tactic to terrorise Anthony Gubbay into resigning. Mushore was followed daily to and from work and when she drove her children to school. CIO agents would telephone Erik Morris, another lawyer, and threaten his wife and children.

But when judgment was passed, Mungwira said all fourteen police involved in the investigation had 'spewed forth untruths' throughout the trial, their records were 'an appalling piece of fiction' and they had conducted themselves 'in a shameless fashion' by torturing the suspects. She found that most of the six were arrested on murder charges days before police had officially found Nkala's body, and acquitted all of the accused.[15]

By the time real change comes to Zimbabwe, there could be few judges on the bench with the courage of Sandra Mungwira or Lawrence Kamocha, and it will take years to rebuild an independent judiciary. In the short term, it may be necessary to borrow judges from other democracies like India, Botswana or South Africa.

But, ahead of change, it would be useful to make contact with Zimbabwean lawyers working in exile and to identify those who might be willing to come home.

There are also a number of staunch human rights lawyers in Zimbabwe, like Beatrice Mtetwa, who defended journalist Andrew Meldrum ahead of his deportation in 2003. Beatrice has worked on countless high-profile cases and would bring a wealth of experience to the bench.

Changing legislation, the judiciary and the nature of policing in Zimbabwe could take years and might need a platoon of lawyers. But the MDC has promised wholesale reform in its first year of government. If the party came to power and kept its word, this would be one of the few times that Africa had seen freedom enshrined in both the law and the constitution.

Across the Limpopo, research published in Johannesburg in November 2004 showed that as many as 25 per cent of South African Police Service members were functionally illiterate, making it hard for some officers to record evidence or even deal with basic enquiries from the public.[16]

But with Zimbabwe's high literacy rate, finding able recruits for a new service should not be hard. There are still many people like Constable Richard Phiri, who used to help me rescue snakes in Budiriro: brave, bright, courteous and willing to do whatever it takes to serve the public.

With officers like Richard – and with good policy and a little planning – Zimbabwe could once again become a safe and law-abiding nation.

4

Food, Glorious Food

Zimbabwe's land reform programme has achieved neither fairness nor productivity. Instead it has virtually destroyed agricultural capacity while simply rewarding senior ZANU-PF, military and business circles with a windfall of land they often neglect.

– International Crisis Group, Brussels, 2004[1]

IN THE HISTORY OF EVERY COUNTRY, THERE ARE ONE OR two events that have passed into common understanding. In the United States, the War of Independence, with its 4 435 American casualties, is a rallying point for people of all races – even new immigrants – and you only have to be there on the Fourth of July to understand how deeply that statement of sovereignty has shaped the nation.

British people take pride in the stoic efforts that saw them through World War II, and especially the Blitz, and Koreans still remember the suffering that marked the years of Japanese occupation. Yet, when Americans light their fireworks, they don't curse the English, who in turn welcome thousands of German visitors every year, while Japan is Korea's second largest trading partner.

The same is true of Zimbabwe. More than half the population was either not born at the time of the civil war in the 1970s or is too young to remember it. But everyone is aware that a conflict took place and cognisant that, when the whites arrived in 1890, they subjugated the local population, occupied their land and stole their cattle without compensation.

This doesn't translate to a hatred of whites. An estimated 70 per cent of blacks now live in urban areas or in exile, and few seek tracts of land for their own use. But when you talk to people, it becomes evident that a significant number believe the injustice suffered by their ancestors should be recognised, if only through an apology. Beyond that, the so-called land debate is a minor issue, and in the twenty-first century, black culture is more about consumer goods and cellphones than raising crops.

How, then, did the cry for land come to be so closely associated with ZANU-PF and the world's perception of Zimbabwe? The answer can be summed up in one word: desperation. In 2000, when Robert Mugabe faced defeat at the polls, he tore open wounds that had long since healed and launched a campaign based on prejudice.

Hate has long been used to rally the masses. Hitler's policy on Jews played a key part in his rise to power. If no Arabs lived in France, right-wing politician Jean-Marie le Pen might struggle to win a seat on a town council, let alone enough votes to become a run-off candidate for the presidency. And how would the bumbling National Party in apartheid South Africa have stayed in power if not for the cries of *swart gevaar* (black danger), a warning that democracy would herald a government of savages ready to murder the peace-loving whites in their beds?

In Sudan and Rwanda, politicians have exploited ethnicity to the point of genocide, with no shortage of volunteers eager to rub out the menace of those who were surely responsible for whatever ailed the nation. But for the campaign to work, three factors are usually present:

- the media is under state control;
- the argument appeals to those with least education;
- some amount of *real* anger is present.

Hitler spoke to the unemployed and the working class who

saw Jews – many of them descended from East European immigrants – prospering in a Germany that was on its knees after World War I.

In France, there was genuine concern about the high number of Arabs taking lowly paid jobs from French workers, but a free press meant that Le Pen's simplistic message of 'France for the French' was questioned by writers who failed to see the argument in black and white.

Rwanda was not so lucky. The Tutsis, traditionally advantaged under Belgian rule, were generally more prosperous than the largely illiterate Hutu majority. When the Hutu-led dictatorship lost popularity in the late 1980s, they ignited that resentment, with tragic results. The Rwandan media, and especially one Hutu radio station in Kigali, fanned the genocide, broadcasting the location of homes, schools and churches where Tutsis were hiding.

In South Africa, where the government controlled television and all but two radio stations, internal opposition to apartheid was possible through the newspapers, which were all in private hands. Ironically, at the height of state repression, the country probably had the freest press in Africa.

But while human rights activists railed against media censorship in South Africa, they were largely silent in 1981 when Mugabe nationalised the press, and those who failed to speak out must bear some responsibility for what followed. Without the media, indications are that Mugabe would have lost power within a decade, or by 1995 at the latest. Instead, the challenge was delayed, and when it came in 2000, the president followed the well-trodden path of tyrants, drawing the debate as a Venn diagram,[2] with the struggling masses in one circle and their heartless oppressors in another.

If only the white minority could be gone, the evil they had wrought in the form of poverty and unemployment would disappear. And central to white power was the huge amount of 'stolen' land they occupied, at the expense of the poor.

Mugabe's control of the media – especially after the government banned the independent *Daily News* in 2003 – made it hard to counter the message, but many analysts ignore the other factor: there was *some* resentment against white Zimbabweans.

As an African, I have my own view of the problem. I speak Shona fairly fluently, and white friends often remark how much they'd like to chat with black people in their own language. Yet few have made the effort.

People of English descent living in Argentina speak Spanish, most white Kenyans are fluent in Swahili, and expatriate Britons who have bought holiday homes on the Algarve may *fala Portugués* after a style. Yet the majority of white Zimbabweans would not know more than a dozen words in the local tongue (which puts them ten words ahead of white South Africans).

Perhaps the problem is that when Africa was colonised, black people sought to emulate Western culture in dress, style, food, economy and even language, while the native way of life was less seductive, and few of the newcomers aspired to a mud hut. Maybe that set the pattern for what is now perceived as white elitism or separateness, which is, itself, emulated by wealthy black people, some of whom look down on their own working class.

Years ago, in Sydney, I watched a debate on anti-Semitism. On one side, a local rabbi complained that his people were 'gently excluded' from society, not by law, not overtly, but by a national attitude that Jews were not quite as Australian as the Anglo-Saxon majority.

'People don't mix with Jews, they don't want us in the mainstream,' the rabbi said. 'Instead, they push us to the edge of society, gently, diplomatically, so quietly you would hardly notice.'

His adversary was a loud radio journalist known for her acid comments.

'We don't push you out,' she countered. 'You want your own schools, own clubs, you mix with your own, you marry your own. You exclude yourselves and blame us when you don't fit in.'

The rabbi seemed at a loss to respond, and looked at the largely Jewish audience as if they held the answer.

'That's how we stay Jewish,' he said. 'Without those things, we would disappear.'

Maybe the same applies to whites in Africa.

Race relations in Zimbabwe have always been cordial, and in the 2000 elections, four white MDC candidates – Mike Auret, Roy Bennett, David Coltart and Trudy Stevenson – won seats previously held by black ZANU-PF members of parliament. The biggest majority was achieved in Bennett's constituency, the eastern border district of Chimanimani, where whites made up less than 1 per cent of the voters.

Many farmers and urban residents of European descent had splendid relations with their black workers, friends and colleagues, who saw them as fellow citizens in the fullest sense. But there were some niggling issues that Mugabe was able to exploit.

Born in 1984, Luckmore Ndoro is typical of Zimbabwe's new 'double-E' generation: eloquent and educated. He finished school in 2000 with good passes at O-level, but his family couldn't find the fees for two years of A-level tuition. Even so, he is more literate and numerate than many his age leaving the state school system in Britain, and after more than sixty job applications, he landed a trainee post selling short-term insurance in Harare.

'I am somewhere between the Nose Brigade and the Bin-2s,' he told me during an interview in January 2005. For those not familiar with the jargon, the Nose Brigade are youngsters who shun Shona or Ndebele, speaking only English to each other in a tone their parents describe as nasal. It also means a snob, nose in the air, interchangeable with *salala* or 'salads', the term for young girls who diet on greens and look sideways at *sadza*, the traditional maize porridge that is Zimbabwe's staple food.

Bin-2s are those who have travelled abroad: been to London, been to Cape Town. Luckmore had travelled only as far as Johannesburg, which doesn't count, since most Zimbabweans now have family in the city they call 'Mbare South'.

'I want to finish my education,' Luckmore says, 'but that will have to wait. Right now I'm making good money for my age, but my dad died last year so I'm keeping Mum and paying fees for two brothers and a sister still at school.'

Luckmore's older sister, who lives in Johannesburg, had introduced us while he was visiting over New Year after I told her I wanted to interview young blacks about their attitude to whites. This is what Luckmore told me:

> My generation knows that the war happened. We've had it worked into us at school. My parents lived through that time, but they never talk about it much. All they tell us is how good life was back then, low prices, free health and so on.
>
> So I don't think there's a hangover from those days. And I've got black and white friends, but I don't really think of their colour. They're just Patrick, Justin, Liz and Tensin. And aside from Tensin, most have got white names, though Justin is black. A lot of whites my age speak a crappy Shona they learnt in school, but we all talk English anyway.
>
> I think if black people have any hang-ups about whites, it's with the over-forties who still talk down to us. Chatting with the friendly natives. They call themselves African and pretend we're all equal, but they huddle together at their dinners and at clubs: us-and-them. I doubt many have

> ridden an ET (minibus taxi used mostly by blacks) or visited friends in the townships. They just live in their own world, and I find that sad. I don't hate them for it, but some people do.

For those who would like to read further on the war, its causes and complexities, I suggest the novels *Harvest of Thorns* and *The Rain Goddess*. In non-fiction, consider *Selous Scouts: Top Secret War* and *None But Ourselves*.[3]

Funwell Taruvinga, twenty-four years older than Luckmore, was twenty when the war ended. He lost his stepfather, a sergeant in the Rhodesia African Rifles, and two brothers, who were guerrilla fighters with Mugabe's ZANLA. His father had been killed in a landmine explosion near Kariba when Funwell was eight. He, too, had got over the war, but was not as accommodating of whites:

> I've been in eight jobs since independence, most of them working for whites. They are good employers and pay on time. Working for other blacks is dodgy – sometimes they pay you, some months it's late. There are good black bosses, but if you're unlucky like I was in two jobs, the business goes broke or the boss runs away from his debts and you are left with nothing.
>
> I started as a trainee draughtsman in Mutare, and I've worked in Bulawayo, Hwange and Harare, as a guard, a driver and now I'm a messenger at a parastatal.
>
> I think whites don't like talking to blacks. Before independence, it was not allowed for us to live in white areas or even go to white schools or hospitals. That has changed, but most whites have never learnt Shona and they talk to you like you're a junior, a naughty child who needs to be steered so-so. They don't ask you to do something, they want to tell you how to do it as well, even when you know the job better than they do.

And the farmers were the worst. I've got brothers who used to work on white farms and I was also there as a driver in 1992. Now my brothers are all unemployed. One has a plot near Gweru, but he's struggling. Life was better when the whites had the farms, but it wasn't good. The farmers were rude, loud, harsh with their words, like you were a dog. The farmers' clubs were for whites only and they never mixed with us. We gave them friendship, but they never tried to be close with us.

Some farmers set up schools or clinics, but from what I saw, they were few. Many black kids worked in the tobacco barns; there was plenty of child labour.

Without whites, we cannot run the farms. I know that, and it has been proved. Without blacks, the whites also could not farm, but to them, our labour was just another cost like seed or fertiliser.

I don't support Mugabe and I cry because people are starving. The farm invasions were wrong. I didn't participate in them and I would never do that. But I don't have pity for the farmers. For the good ones, it was sad, but for most of them, I feel nothing. That's how much they used to feel for us. They were just rude old men who knew how to grow crops.

Rude *old* men?

Even without Mugabe, white farming was on the road to extinction. Just as young blacks were deserting rural life in search of jobs in the city, so the sons and daughters of white farming families went to boarding school and, after A-level, the typical pattern was university in South Africa and a job in that country or overseas.

But farming colleges, even universities, were packed with young black men and women learning agriculture, and by 2000, 20 per cent of commercial farmers were black. In my view, within two decades white farmers would have been a minority and the sector would still be thriving.

My assertion is not the product of research, because I couldn't find any hard figures, but countless visits to farming areas, and especially to the all-white farmers' clubs, revealed an ageing population, drinking together, playing tennis, squash, snooker and darts, a welcoming community of true Africans, tied to the soil and in love with Zimbabwe. But few of their off-spring were queuing up to work the land.

As things stand in 2005, aerial photographs of rural Zimbabwe show bush encroachment where, mile upon mile, no one is tilling the fields that used to generate maize, wheat, tobacco and cotton. In other areas, there is wholesale deforestation, but little new agriculture. Small-scale farmers have deserted their original land in the tribal areas and taken a similar tract on a commercial farm, but have not increased their output.

By the government's own figures, at the end of 2004, just over 150 000 families had been resettled, but only 60 per cent of the plots on offer had been taken up. Now do the maths. If you generously allow for six people in every family, that's 900 000 at most, or, out of a population of 12 to 14 million, less than 8 per cent. And many of the plot-holders have abandoned their new fields and headed back to the city.[4]

While some people did need land, the wholesale demand claimed by Mugabe never existed, and with vacant and under-utilised farms and land already in state hands, there was more than enough to meet demand.

The whole issue could have been settled after independence. More than forty farms around Mount Darwin and Centenary became vacant, and some blacks were resettled in the area, but without help from government they confined themselves to subsistence agriculture, while some managed small fields of tobacco and cotton.

What had been an important area for Rhodesia's economy

added virtually zero to Zimbabwe's coffers. For the rest of the country, Mugabe adopted a *laissez-faire* approach to white farmers, while visiting large-scale violence and repression on the black majority, especially in Matabeleland.

In their excellent publication, *Blood and Soil: Land, Politics and Conflict Prevention in Zimbabwe and South Africa*, the Belgian-based International Crisis Group (ICG) summed up the situation that prevailed after 1980:

> At independence, about 6 000 white farmers still occupied some 13.5 million hectares of land, producing around 40 per cent of export earnings and 90 per cent of food for local markets.
>
> When the bureaucracy did try to resettle landless peasants, it became bogged down by organisational problems since as many as twenty-five ministries, departments and parastatals were involved in the complicated process.
>
> There was a debilitating rivalry between the Ministry of Agriculture and Lands, responsible for land acquisition, and the Ministry of Local Government, responsible for settler selection, infrastructure development and support. These conflicts flowed over in forums where the government team tried to negotiate international aid for the programme, and contributed to London's reluctance to fund another phase of resettlement.
>
> Buying the land proved to be the easy part; land purchases accounted for only 44 per cent of the total resettlement costs in the first five years of the programme. Some of the underdeveloped land acquired by the government simply sat idle because it did not seem economical to resettle families on it. Resettlement slowed sharply in the late 1980s, dropping below 5 000 families a year.
>
> In July 1990, agriculture minister Witness Mangwende unveiled a new plan to resettle 1 100 families on 5 million hectares. As 54 000 families had already been resettled on

> 3.3 million hectares, Mangwende was in essence restating an old goal of 162 000 families on roughly 9 million hectares. Purchases no longer had to be in foreign currency and the government could force unwilling farmers to sell their land.

But, secure in power and with the economy doing well enough to stave off revolt, ZANU-PF felt little need to accommodate the rural poor. Instead, they focused on the urban economy and their own enrichment, with military forays into Mozambique and later the Congo, each providing a windfall for ministers and their business colleagues, who were able to supply goods to the army and, in the Congo, embezzle spoils in the form of diamonds, cobalt and timber.

Handing out parcels of land was not a priority.

Then came the invasions, and in a call to history Mugabe spoke of past injustice, claiming that stolen fields could never belong to people whose ancestors had dispossessed the masses a hundred years before. The line was that, when Cecil Rhodes sent his Pioneer Column into Matabeleland and Mashonaland, the settlers paid little heed to who owned what, pegging gold claims and marking out farms wherever they liked, driving the local inhabitants off their land at gunpoint and putting down dissent by noose or firing squad.

All true, but not the whole story. In *The Battle for Zimbabwe,*[5] I detailed the country's early history, but it's worth examining again the period from 1890, when European settlers took charge. The Pioneer Column had been financed by Cecil John Rhodes, who, in 1887, had bought up most of the diamond claims in Kimberley, allowing his company, De Beers, to control 90 per cent of global sales. Around the same time, he took a stake in the gold mines around Johannesburg, making him one of the richest men in the world.

But for Rhodes, money was little more than paper; his real dream was to expand British influence from the Cape to Cairo, and the first task was to secure south-central Africa, which was bordered by German and Portuguese colonies. Without much effort, those two nations could have claimed what is now Zimbabwe, Zambia and Malawi, forming a belt across the continent and dividing South Africa and the British protectorate of Bechuanaland from the Crown's east African territories of Kenya and Uganda.

The Portuguese had already granted a charter to the Companhia da Moçambique, a private firm that Lisbon had engaged to mine the gold fields of the Manyika and Korekore people in eastern Zimbabwe. Their traders and marshals had penetrated as far as Mount Darwin, 140 kilometres north-east of present-day Harare.

Then there was the Transvaal, founded in the mid-1800s by the Boers, African-born descendants of Dutch settlers who had trekked north from the Cape. The Boers (farmers in Dutch) were led by the cantankerous Paul Kruger, who was anxious to preserve his people's independence. Rhodes feared that Kruger might establish a foothold across the Limpopo River, which marked the boundary between the Transvaal and Matabeleland. But if Germany, Portugal, Kruger, Rhodes or the Portuguese wanted to take the area between the Zambezi and Limpopo, they would have to deal with the Matabele.

King Mzilikazi had died in 1868, and was succeeded by his son, Lobengula, who continued to rule the Shona, raiding their crops and cattle and killing those who resisted.

The idea of settling the territory was spurred by exaggerated reports from some explorers who, having seen the ancient ruined city of Great Zimbabwe, believed they had stumbled upon King Solomon's mines. This, surely, was the fabled land of Ophir, whose riches would rival or even outshine the deep gold seams of Johannesburg.

Rhodes moved quickly, engaging the help of David

Livingstone's brother-in-law, John Moffat, who had grown up in Africa and knew Lobengula well, and sent him to negotiate. Once Moffat had softened up the king, Rhodes asked his old friend, Charles Rudd, to do the deal. Lobengula could neither read nor write, but on 29 October 1888, in exchange for a promise of protection from other colonisers, guns to further subdue the Shona, a boat on the Zambezi and various other gifts, he signed over mining rights in his colony of Mashonaland.

The king agonised over the deal and had many a change of heart, but with the concession in hand, Rhodes went to England and sold shares in his new British South Africa Company, the sole purpose of which was to colonise the land that would soon be named Rhodesia in his honour.

A military force, the British South Africa Police, was recruited to lead the way, and on 12 September 1890, having ridden from Kimberley, the column of 500 volunteers, support staff and prospectors raised the Union flag at a place they named Fort Salisbury, after the British foreign secretary.

A flagpole still stands on the spot next to Africa Unity Square on Second Avenue in central Harare.

After one last muster, the men bombshelled, each determined to peg off the best claims. In his book, *Pioneers of Mashonaland*, Adrian Darter recalls what happened: 'Extravagant reports of alluvial gold and rich reefs were the order of the day. Old workings were eagerly sought for and, in that way, many a Shona field was pegged off. Rushes, stark, staring mad rushes possessed the prospectors.'

In a matter of weeks, the BSAC had established bases all over Mashonaland and built surprisingly good relations with the local population. However, the initial success did not last. Salisbury experienced unusually heavy rains, which made movement around the town difficult, let alone across a country that had no roads. With the water came malaria, and those who managed to fight their way through the difficulties found little gold to support the original idea that they would all be rich.

Mail and supplies were bogged down, and the contract the men had signed with the BSAC, in which they promised to hand over 50 per cent of all gold to the company, would bankrupt even those who had made reasonable finds. There was no alluvial gold to be panned from the rivers or picked up as nuggets, and deeper veins needed capital equipment and years of work to extract. So the men fell back on the next promise of wealth: farming.

Land was marked out with no regard to the Shona, who had taken to living in the hills, coming down to the valleys when they were sure the Matabele were not around. This gave the impression that vast areas were not under permanent claim.

There had been no trouble with Lobengula, who had honoured the concession, even though the terms granted only mining rights and fell far short of permission to occupy the country.

But, as more land was taken by the settlers, war broke out, first with the Matabele and then the Shona. Maxim guns pitted against spears and single-shot rifles ensured a settler victory, and by the time Rhodes died in 1902, the Matabele nation, monarchy and all, had been snuffed out. For the survivors and the Shona alike there was no other option but to work for the new rulers.

In 1919, the Privy Council in London ruled that all land under BSAC control belonged to the Crown, and in 1922 Britain agreed to sell it to the new government of Southern Rhodesia for £2 300 000, without recognising prior ownership by the San, Shona or Matabele.

Various commissions marked out just over half the agricultural land for the exclusive use of blacks, but with Western medicine, and especially the control of malaria and sleeping sickness, the population grew rapidly, and by the 1960s the Tribal Trust Lands, or TTLs, were crowded.

At the same time more young blacks were being educated and moving to town in search of jobs. With Zimbabwe's independence in 1980 and expansion of the school system under the first Mugabe government, a wholesale shift took place.

In 1901, Rhodesia's population had been 712 600. By 1937, it stood at approximately 1.35 million, and more than 3 million in 1970, including about 300 000 whites and a largely rural black population. In 1982, the headcount was just over 7 million, and by 1992 the number had ballooned to 10.4 million, with almost half living in urban areas.

By 2004, the population had almost doubled since independence, with perhaps a quarter of Zimbabwe's people living on foreign soil. More telling, the number of residents in Harare had grown by more than 500 per cent, and smaller centres such as Bulawayo, Mutare, Gweru and Masvingo had also mushroomed.

But while the government had done much to provide its citizens with the education that inevitably took them to town, no provision was made for the needs of an educated workforce. Two decades after Mugabe came to power, unemployment stood at between 60 and 80 per cent. And while food prices escalated, a string of corruption scandals tarnished the government's reputation; the independent press ran stories about cabinet ministers buying new cars, sending children to school abroad, and taking their families on binge shopping trips to New York, London and Paris.

Revolutions are invariably led by the urban poor: France in 1789, Russia in 1917, India in Gandhi's fight for independence, the struggle against apartheid in South Africa. Zimbabwe was no different, and the disenchanted youth – educated, urban-dwelling, and either unemployed or working on low wages – demanded change. By 2000, their call led to the formation of the MDC, but nowhere in the riots and strikes was there any mention of land. On the contrary, a series of national opinion polls conducted in 2000 showed that, on a list of ten priorities, people rated resettlement somewhere between seven and nine.[6]

In his oratory, however, Mugabe was able to call on history to make his claim that the suffering his people were complaining about had not been wrought by his government; at the heart of the problem was the land stolen a century before by white scoundrels whose descendants still lived apart from the majority in lofty seclusion. And he would now right that wrong, nationalise those farms and hand them over to the masses.

Not many bought the claim, but with the media under state control, the police and army politicised, and the courts castrated, the government had its way, and by 2004, 90 per cent of white-owned farms had been confiscated. In many cases, farmers were removed violently from their land by government-sponsored teams of war veterans and local youths in pay of the state. An estimated 600 000 agricultural workers and their families – a total of more than 1.5 million people – were also evicted and rendered homeless. And here was another clue to the real agenda. Farm workers, with their cash income and a lifestyle better than those on communal land, formed a major part of the MDC's rural voter base, and displacing them could only benefit ZANU-PF in future elections. But, having been taken, the best land was kept aside.

Justice for Agriculture, a commercial farmers' group, released a list in late February 2003 that identified 1 000 farms, their location and size, and the names of the new farmers and former owners. The land on the list approached 2 million hectares, with an average farm size of 1 975 hectares.

Mugabe's relatives, numerous ZANU-PF parliamentarians, high-ranking military and police officials, senior civil servants, commissioners, provincial governors, members of the Central Intelligence Organisation, councillors, war veterans and businessmen loyal to the party had all received farms.[7]

But, since land was not behind Zimbabwe's poverty and unemployment, nationalising it did nothing to relieve the pain. Instead, the already burdened population now faced hunger and economic collapse, which made their prior hardship seem like a time of plenty.

Before considering how one might restore agriculture in Zimbabwe, it is important to understand how far the sector has fallen from its erstwhile level as Africa's second largest food producer. Eddie Cross is an economist and a member of the MDC planning committee. In December 2004, he summed up the state of farming:

> After four years of chaos, we have about 600 000 people partially settled on 12 million hectares of land that once supported 2 million people (farmers, farm workers and their families). The same land now employs about 60 000 people in paid jobs, where once we employed 350 000. Rural incomes have plummeted from about three times the national average to well below that level.
>
> Before the 'land reform', we were the third largest exporter of tobacco in the world, we were the largest beef exporter in Africa, and major producers of cotton, milk, sugar, fruit and horticultural products. The industry generated a third of Zimbabwe's national employment, half its exports and fed a population of 11 million.
>
> Today we have 75 per cent of our population dependent on food handouts or imports; we are unable to supply our needs for vegetable oils, milk, meat and fruit. And our food prices have risen to the highest in the region from being the lowest in Africa in 1997.

Cross's observations are backed up by figures from the Economist Intelligence Unit (EIU), noting that real gross domestic product shrank 0.7 per cent in 1999, 4.9 per cent in 2000, 8.4 per cent in 2001 and 13 per cent in 2002. It fell another 13.2 per cent in 2003, and nearly 10 per cent in 2004.

In the EIU's opinion, 'There is now little constructive policy planning, merely ad hoc crisis management, coupled with a hefty dose of wishful thinking.'

And the pain was not only felt at home. A South African economist estimated that Zimbabwe's collapse cost the region $2.6 billion between 2000 and 2002, with much of this due to cancelled exports and failure to pay for services.[8]

By 2004, Zimbabwe had the world's highest inflation rate and the fastest-shrinking economy; foreign exchange reserves dwindled to a mere $60 million, and external debt reached $4.1 billion. As early as August 2001, the World Food Programme (WFP) warned of an 'exceptional food emergency', and began formulating plans to deal with looming shortages. By March 2002, the WFP indicated that more than half a million people needed food aid. That same year, the wheat harvest was 170 000 tons, well below the 300 000-ton average.

By 2004, less than 10 per cent of arable land was producing some sort of grain. The commercial beef herd had declined from 1.2 million to fewer than 150 000, with foot-and-mouth disease a serious problem and little money available for vaccines.[9]

Whomever the task falls to, rebuilding the agricultural sector is a challenge not to be wished on your worst enemy. Even when freedom comes, it's likely there will still be an urgent need to feed people. Grain and protein will need to be imported for up to four or five years while farming gets back on its feet.

With law and order and transparent government in place, and food no longer being used as a weapon or propaganda tool by the ruling party, it would be possible to set up a fair system of handouts, while at the same time ensuring that progress was made towards commercial farming.

A widely touted idea is the setting up of a land commission to survey the former commercial farms and the communal fields, chiefs' land, protected areas, national parks and private game reserves. The ICG recommended that this body should:

- have a clear mandate and be ready to swing into action quickly;
- be given a timetable for achieving its goals;
- conduct a comprehensive inventory of land based on who owns what, status of redistribution, compensation paid to original owners, and whether or not farms are being used productively;
- organise land tribunals to mediate claims on the ground, as well as considerable field staff to assist the process;
- incorporate broad public input;
- develop a compensation formula for farms that were seized;
- develop new enterprises, making sure new farmers have access to needed expertise, while establishing incentives for commercial farmers to return to their land;
- set the parameters of a new law to govern land reform.

Zimbabwe had an excellent system of record-keeping, so it should be possible to establish the prior status of any land and correlate this with current use.

Farms given to friends of ZANU-PF would have to be taken over by the land commission, pending return to their original owners. Should the latter be unwilling to return or have left the country, the farms could be sold at best commercial value and some of the money used to compensate the previous owners.

This has recent precedent in Kenya. President Daniel arap Moi's Kenya African National Union (KANU) lost power in 2002, having ruled the country since independence in 1963.

The new government ordered a land audit, and millions of hectares were found to have been handed out to KANU ministers, officials, their families and supporters. Slowly, the land was taken back. This included tracts belonging to Moi.

In 2004, an inquiry launched by the new lands minister, Amos Kimunya, revealed that game reserve land, state forests, bus parks, government houses, military and trust lands, settlement schemes and even cemeteries had been dished out to allies of the Moi government. Titles were revoked, and a tribunal was established to deal with restitution.[10]

In Zimbabwe, when seized farms go on sale, the new government would have to decide whether non-citizens should be allowed to buy land. In a world where successful countries have removed ownership restrictions, it seems logical that all bidders should be welcome in order to gain the best price.

Or, as in Mozambique, the land could be sold on ninety-nine-year leasehold. Morocco, which went through a difficult time reclaiming foreign-owned estates after independence from France in 1960, followed this path, leasing nearly 100 000 hectares of cultivated fields in 2004 and 2005.[11]

Any profit from land sales should be ploughed back into the sector. Farms of all types and sizes would need capital during transition. Commercial farmers have had many assets looted, while small-scale growers who have been legitimately resettled would need help to establish themselves.

Failure to support land redistribution with back-up, including plant and veterinary services, fertiliser, health care and schools, sent redistribution off track in the 1980s and would destroy any future effort. The ICG report made a number of other recommendations:

- Records relating to land would have to be regularised and a functioning system of administration rebuilt.
- A valuation exercise should be conducted and, in cases where

new owners acquired farms substantially below market value, they would have to pay in the difference. If they refuse, such farms would revert to the National Land Trust, whether for return to the original owner or redistribution.

- Where land was acquired at a fair price, compensation should be paid to the original owners or they should be offered a new farm.
- Compensation paid to former owners could be derived, in part, from assets seized from individuals associated with the current government and should be distributed to the poorest commercial farmers first.
- Farm workers, in particular, should be targeted for assistance.
- The phase-in of private title for small farmers might encourage a more rational land market.
- Inheritance laws should protect and give ownership rights to women whose husbands have died of AIDS, and to widows in general.
- One of the most immediate needs would be to boost agricultural capacity quickly and enduringly, so that the country does not remain in chronic food deficit. Reviving non-productive farms should be the first priority.
- Peasant farmers resettled on land should be allowed to stay, or, if there were only a few settlers on a large farm that could be better put to commercial use, they could be offered land elsewhere.
- Over a period of ten years, small-scale farmers should show that they are working the land and have made improvements to it. If this is evident, they should be given title.

While the cost of the land redistribution programme would be substantial, the international community currently spends hundreds of millions of dollars on feeding programmes for Zimbabwe. Getting the country back on its feet would ultimately be both cost-effective and more rational, but the new Zimbabwe government, the United Kingdom, the European Union, the United States and the United Nations would have to show both leadership *and* their chequebooks.[12]

One area on which most analysts and writers agree is the need to get rid of Zimbabwe's Grain Marketing Board, or GMB. The law requires that all cereal crops be sold exclusively to the GMB, delivered, offloaded, weighed, stored, resold, reloaded and then moved on. This is not only gross inefficiency, but has also given rise to a thriving black market, with prices three to four times higher than the official rate.

Perpetually on the brink of insolvency, the board is very slow at making payments and, because it ends up selling at below market price, the haemorrhage continues. By manipulating sales, the state has been able to use food as a political weapon, favouring party strongholds and denying maize to areas where voters support the opposition. Since it is illegal for farmers to sell grain directly to consumers or even to milling companies, the GMB has become a powerful tool of oppression. And it is bad economics.

Even the World Food Programme has spoken out against the concept, saying that 'the supply of maize available through the Grain Marketing Board is erratic and scarce'.[13]

To make matters worse, the GMB has been accused of corruption, theft and embezzlement. In May 2004, its former chief executive, Martin Muchero, was charged with smuggling $5 million out of the country and depositing it in a South African bank account for which he was the sole signatory.

Closing down the GMB or setting up a modest, perhaps private-sector organisation, would ease food problems overnight. It is possible that, by the time change comes, other boards will have been set up as the government struggles to control what is left of the economy. In 2005, a Horticultural Marketing

Authority was established, with a sole mandate to market flowers and all other horticultural products. Like the GMB, these new groups should be abolished.[14]

During the chaos, Zimbabwe has lost its traditional markets. Tobacco buyers, unable to fill their needs, have gone elsewhere and signed new contracts. Zambia, Malawi, Mozambique and even Nigeria have poached the white farmers and given them land on which to grow export crops that have then been sold to clients who used to buy from Zimbabwe.

And not only whites have moved to greener pastures. Edwin Moyo, whose $15-million Kondozi Estate in eastern Zimbabwe was raided by the army on Good Friday 2004, re-established himself across the border. 'We will not waste any more time on Kondozi,' he told journalists after the seizure. 'I have been rendered a second-class citizen in my country of origin, so we will take our business elsewhere.'

Kondozi, one of the largest horticultural farms in Africa, stopped all production after the land was nationalised. Instead, the packing shed that was being built to handle fresh produce destined for overseas markets was erected less than fifty kilometres away in Mozambique.

Moyo's company also bought 2 000 hectares under irrigation in Zambia's Gwembe Valley, which he runs jointly with former white commercial farmers. The project received funding from South Africa's Industrial Development Corporation, the Netherlands-based Psom, Britain's Tesco and Barclays Bank International.[15]

China has become the largest single buyer of Zimbabwe's tobacco and could increase its order as output grows.[16] But Kenya has won part of the multimillion-dollar flower market that used to see tons of Zimbabwean roses and carnations flown to Europe annually. Malawi has muscled in on coffee and tea, and South Africa has absorbed the sugar trade. It will take many years to renegotiate deals for Zimbabwean produce.

One area for caution is the handing out of title. Small-scale farmers on new land should be considered for this, but it is my personal view that the old tribal lands should not be cut up into freehold plots. For centuries the chiefs have doled out parcels of land to their subjects, and although the system was politicised under ZANU-PF, it remains workable and should not be abandoned.

For the poorest rural dwellers – often women and the aged – the land on which they grow food is their only asset. Some UN agencies suggest that by granting title, they would be able to use the land as collateral against farm loans. In the first decade of independence, the government granted some 94 000 loans to smallholders, of whom 80 per cent, or 75 000, defaulted. To do the same thing now could see people lose their only means of survival. This happened with tragic results in the Indian state of Andhra Pradesh, where up to 3 000 farmers committed suicide between 1998 and 2004, simply because they could not repay their debts.[17]

Re-establishing Zimbabwe agriculture and getting it right would not only benefit the country and the region, but could also provide a template for the continent.

The demons that need to be overcome in Zimbabwe – corruption, government inefficiency, the use of food and land as political weapons, a breakdown in transport, state monopolies and a bloated bureaucracy – also plague other African countries. Africa remains the only region in the world where per-capita food production has fallen over the past forty years. Most of the continent's poorest people live in rural areas, and although some aid agencies argue that Western trade barriers stop Africa from producing crops for export, it must be remembered that the continent cannot even feed itself.

This is Africa's great challenge. Food security benefits all people, rural and urban, and as Abraham Maslow (1908–1970) described on his famous scale of needs, once people feel sure they have the basics for living – shelter, food and security – they feel more inclined to address their social needs, including the right to freedom.

And thirty years into the future, perhaps a new generation will no longer remember a war as the defining moment of their country's history, but rather see the post-Mugabe era as a time of freedom and renewal, when people truly gained their national and personal independence.

5

Building Freedom

Democracy is an orgy of opinions.
– Pieter-Dirk Uys, South African satirist

SOUTH AFRICA HAS BEEN A MODEL OF PEACEFUL transition. With one of the world's most liberal constitutions and levels of personal freedom that match or exceed those of many European countries, it has surprised the cynics.

Much of the credit goes to apartheid's last head of state, FW de Klerk, and the ANC's first two presidents, Nelson Mandela and Thabo Mbeki, who set up and maintained the structures vital to democracy. But when power changed hands in 1994, South Africa also had a free and diverse media, with the country's newspapers, some radio stations and the pay-TV channel, M-Net, all in private hands.

During apartheid many newspapers were critical of government, and when freedom came they took the same approach to the new order, exposing corruption, theft and neglect. But whereas South Africa inherited a free press, Zimbabwe has repressive laws banning private broadcasts, dictating what journalists may and may not report, and making it all but impossible for the media to operate under anything close to normal conditions.

The BBC and key news agencies have been closed down, and while in theory any of the 150 foreign journalists based in Johannesburg can visit Zimbabwe, their visa applications are often turned down. Changing the law would be only the first step towards building a robust media and a strong civil society, but there are few templates to draw on. Africa has a poor record when it comes to the press.

The 2004 annual report of London-based Freedom House classifies the media in three categories: free, partly free and not free. In sub-Saharan Africa, only seven states made it into the top bracket, with seventeen in the middle group and twenty-four – almost half the countries on the continent – rated as having no freedom for the media.

Two – Kenya and Sierra Leone – had shifted up the scale in the previous twelve months, four had moved down the ladder, and the report notes 'dire conditions in Zimbabwe, Tunisia and Eritrea'.[1]

Another report, issued by Paris-based *Reporters Sans Frontières* (RSF), or Reporters Without Borders, was just as bad. Out of 167 countries surveyed, thirty-three African states fell in the lower half of the list, and none made the top 20. South Africa was 26th, while Zimbabwe appeared near the bottom, at 156, worse than Libya at 129 or Eritrea's dismal 132.

On both lists, the worst offenders all had a long history of repressing the media.[2]

Rhodesia's first newspaper, the *Mashonaland Herald*, was founded in Salisbury in 1891, a year after whites settled in the country. The British South Africa Company censored the content to make sure stories were not critical of its activities, but after attaining self-government in 1923, the *Rhodesia Herald*, as it became, suffered little interference and formed a common stable with the *Sunday Mail* (1935), and, in Bulawayo, the *Chronicle* (1894) and *Sunday News* (1930). On the eastern border, the *Umtali Post* (1894) covered Manicaland.

The first signs of trouble emerged with the Unilateral Declaration of Independence (UDI) on 11 November 1965, when the government passed laws allowing it to remove any story from a newspaper ahead of publication. At first, the papers left white spaces to show where reports had been excised, until a further law made that illegal.

In 1981, Mugabe nationalised the press with a loan from the civilian government in Nigeria. Newspapers that had been restricted under the old regime were crippled even further. All the editors were fired, and new ones, appointed by the state, were required to support the ruling party. At election time, opposition groups struggled to even buy advertising space. The only dissent came from the weeklies.

The *Financial Gazette*, originally set up by the Rhodesian government and later bought out by Clive Wilson and Clive Murphy, has been owned by black investors since the early 1990s. Printed on pink paper, like the *Financial Times* in London, it carries a mix of business and politics, and its senior staff included the head of the Zimbabwe Union of Journalists, Basildon Peta, until he went into exile in 2002 and began working for the *Star* in Johannesburg and as Africa correspondent for the London *Independent*.

The *Independent*, set up in 1996 by Clive Murphy, Trevor Ncube and Clive Wilson to compete with the *Gazette*, comes out on Friday and carries more hard news and less finance. It is now owned by Ncube, who, in 2002, bought the *Mail & Guardian* in South Africa.

On weekends, there is the *Standard*, a Sunday tabloid launched in 1997, also owned by Ncube and, until 1991, edited by Mark Chavunduka, the son of a former ZANU-PF member of parliament. In 1999, Mark and his colleague, Ray Choto, made headlines around the world when they were arrested and tortured by the army and CIO in an effort to make them reveal the sources behind a story about an aborted coup.

At the end of 1999, the first private daily since 1981 was

founded by Geoff Nyarota, a former editor of the *Umtali Post* and the *Chronicle*, who had been removed from office for printing a story on corruption in cabinet. The *Daily News*, financed largely from abroad with the help of veteran British publisher Derek Smail, quickly outsold the *Herald*, and is largely credited with the MDC's success in the 2000 election.

In response, information minister Jonathan Moyo, who had been jeered in parliament as 'Mugabe's Goebbels', passed laws requiring that newspapers and their staff be licenced, with stiff penalties for journalists whose facts were disputed by the state. It also became a crime to 'insult the president'.

By 2004, the *Daily News* had been banned when Moyo refused to grant it a licence, insisting that the paper had been late in lodging its application. But if newspapers had it tough, the electronic media fared even worse.

In November 1960, Rhodesia had established Africa's first television service to complement a stable of English and local language radio stations. But with UDI, editorial independence fell away, and in 1980 Mugabe moved quickly to put his most trusted aides in charge of news and programming at the Zimbabwe Broadcasting Corporation.

By 2000, a lack of investment in the medium and the flight of staff had seen a collapse in quality and content, and efforts to free the airwaves were stifled at birth.

In December 1998, ZBC radio broadcaster Gerry Jackson allowed callers to her popular morning show to go on air with news that downtown Harare was thick with tear gas after food riots had sparked running battles with police. Parts of the city had been cordoned off, people were stuck in their cars, and Gerry warned drivers to avoid the CBD. The information ministry had not yet made the riots public, and Gerry was accused of 'spreading alarm and despondency' … and fired!

Undeterred, she set up a private radio station. Traditional

wisdom held that this was illegal, but when Gerry took her case to the high court, she was free to proceed after winning a ruling based on the fact that Section 20 (1) of the constitution guaranteed freedom of expression, and no laws had been passed banning private stations. Within a week, she and a small group of compéres were on air under the name of Capital Radio, beamed out of a makeshift studio in the Monomotapa Hotel in Harare.

Days later, Mugabe used his powers of decree to make it illegal for anyone except the state to own a transmitter, and armed police stormed the studio, confiscating tapes and equipment. When the court ordered the police to return the goods they defied the ruling, and Gerry decided to move the entire operation to the safety of London. Her team included some of Zimbabwe's best-known voices: Georgina Godwin, Mandy Mundawarara – the first black newsreader on the old Rhodesian television service – Tererayi Karimakwenda, Violet Gonda, John Matinde and Richard Allfred.

On 19 September 2001, SWRA (Shortwave Radio Africa) went on air. A year later, their listenership in Zimbabwe and among exiles in South Africa had mushroomed to the point where Attorney-General Patrick Chinamasa called for the arrest of any person linked to the station. In response, listeners dubbed it Radio Manyoka, a Shona word for diarrhoea, the ailment, they said, that it gave Chinamasa and others in cabinet.

Short wave works best at night, and SWRA broadcasts from 6 p.m. to 9 p.m. local time, with a mix of hard news, interviews, and social issue programmes on AIDS, women's rights and the pain of family life in a country with nearly a third of its population living in exile. By March 2005, the station was also transmitting on medium wave.

Ultimately, Gerry would like to see SWRA set up as a private news station on the FM band in a free Zimbabwe. But the real challenge, she says, will be to reform the ZBC after forty years of state control and two decades of neglect. 'That's going to take more money than I think even the donor countries and NGOs realise,' she said over coffee in a small restaurant near her North London studios, where I called to see her in September 2004. 'The ZBC still has excellent equipment that could be dusted off and repaired. That's the easy bit. The hard task is recruiting staff. There was a time in the 1970s and 1980s when the corporation had some of the best technicians in Africa, people with enormous skill and experience. There were camera operators, sound engineers, even make-up artists for television, plus a team of broadcasters, black and white, who would be quite at home on the BBC.'

She continued: 'But as standards fell and content turned from entertainment to propaganda, people left. And of course, wages never kept pace with inflation. So you would need to recruit a whole new team, bearing in mind that most of the journalists still at ZBC are skilled only in toeing the government line. People who left and are now in South Africa or overseas could be lured back, but you would have to pay them in foreign currency.'

Ahead of any reform, the legal framework would need to be changed, and, according to Trevor Ncube, this lies at the heart of the issue. While he still owns the *Standard* and *Independent* in Harare, Ncube spends much of his time in South Africa, running that country's premier weekly paper, the *Mail & Guardian*. The *M&G*, as it's known, was set up in 1985 and soon built a reputation for tackling corruption in business and government. Overstaffed, poorly managed and on the point of closure when he bought it, the *M&G* was breaking more stories than ever and turning a profit within two years of Ncube's purchase.

'For me, the fundamental issues are a new constitution and

a very strong bill of rights,' he told me in February 2005, when we talked about the challenges of rebuilding Zimbabwe's media. 'South Africa's Constitution would be a good model, but the rights of citizens have to be written down. And there must be guarantees for freedom of the press, freedom of association and expression, and the neutrality of any state-owned media. These issues must be totally non-negotiable, as strong as America's First Amendment. And, once it is sealed, changing the constitution should require at least a 75 per cent vote in parliament, even a referendum. In Zimbabwe, we have learnt these things the hard way, and we don't want to see the same tyranny at any time in the future, so we need very strong provisions to defend our freedom.'

Whatever the law, those in power may still try their luck, but good legislation makes it a lot harder. In August 2004, the democratically elected government of Brazil announced plans to set up a national council to 'orient, discipline and monitor' journalists, who would be obliged to register with the body. Penalties for violations of the council's rules or rulings would range from fines to a reporter's registration being cancelled, effectively barring the offender from working in the media.

President Luiz Inácio Lula da Silva also proposed a National Cinema and Audiovisual Agency, which would have the authority to judge whether films and television programmes were producing work that was 'in harmony with the goals of social development of the country'. No surprise that, at the time, Da Silva's government was rocked by allegations of corruption and irregularities, all widely reported in the press.

Judges, magistrates, human rights groups and, of course, journalists, shouted down the proposals as the greatest attack on free speech since Brazil's military dictatorship gave way to democracy in 1985.

The chief justice of the supreme court, Edison Vidigal, said the measure displayed 'a certain terrorism', and also suggested it was unconstitutional. In response, the president's chief advisor on communications issues, Luiz Gushiken, declared that 'In a society, no right is absolute,' and called on the media to adopt a 'positive agenda' and avoid 'exploiting contradictions that foment discord and ego conflicts'. But in no time the government changed its stance, saying that all it had had in mind was a professional body that would be run by the journalists themselves, similar to organisations that control doctors, lawyers and accountants.[3]

The difference in Brazil was that a free press already existed, ready to challenge the bill. In Zimbabwe, with print and broadcast under party control, the government can pass laws at will, and journalists have to sell the new policy to the public or lose their jobs.

Basildon Peta believes that a warning should be sent to a future Zimbabwe government. 'Of course press freedom should be enshrined in the constitution,' he says, 'and current legislation must be scrapped. But I would also abolish the ministry of information; the state does not need a minister in cabinet to oversee the press. However, we can't leave it there. If it is legally possible, people who played an active role in the demise of media freedom, including Jonathan Moyo, should be arrested and put on trial. You need to set an example, so that others might think twice before they go that route.'

Moyo was fired by Mugabe in February 2005, and won a seat in the March election as an independent, but a strong body of opinion holds that he should still be called to account by a future government.

Beyond basic freedom lies the issue of privilege. In Sweden, for example, journalistic sources are sacrosanct, but this is not the case in all European countries … or in South Africa. The apartheid government relied on Section 205 of the Criminal Procedure Act, which can require any person involved in a case, with the sole exception of lawyers working on a particular case, to give evidence if called as a witness.

Doctors, mental health workers, journalists, even priests hearing confession may be compelled to divulge what they know about a crime. No exceptions, and journalists have often been caught in the net, even since 1994.

'There have been changes to the Act and the way it is enforced,' says Janet Mackenzie, a director of Cliffe Dekker Attorneys, who has handled several cases under Section 205. 'And with local and international precedents placing ever more emphasis on the independence of journalists, the law will evolve. But as things stand it is still on the books, and journalists can be fined or jailed if they don't hand over notes or reveal even the most confidential of sources. Zimbabwe should learn from that and follow a better model.'

But, having established the framework, how would a new government run the ZBC and the state-owned press? Peta's view is that they shouldn't. 'There are plenty of bread-and-butter issues for government, but this is not one of them. It is no coincidence that in the world's most prosperous democracies, the state does not busy itself running the media. There may be a case for the ZBC to remain a public broadcaster, but with total independence. However, the newspapers should be sold off as quickly as possible.'

Ncube concurs: 'The government has no business being in print media, none at all, and all their papers should be sold. No matter who runs Zimbabwe, while the state owns the press, there will be a temptation to use it as a weapon. So the sale should be a priority. The airwaves are slightly different. I would want to see the ZBC remain a public broadcaster, but well protected from interference. The reason for not selling it is that the corporation must serve all Zimbabweans, whereas a private company will only support those functions that are financially viable.'

According to Ncube, 'Only a public broadcaster will cover a cattle show in a far-off village or make radio programmes in minority languages like Venda or Shangaan. But, by structuring the board correctly, ensuring total independence for journalists and perhaps borrowing from overseas models like the Australian Broadcasting Corporation, which is government funded but has no allegiance to any party, it would be possible to create a world-class radio and TV service. But private stations should be able to set up in competition, as we have seen in South Africa.'

Geoff Nyarota, founding editor of the *Daily News*, is now with the John F Kennedy School of Government at Harvard University in Massachusetts. He believes that with the advent of private broadcasting, the market would become a force for good: 'An atmosphere of strong professional competition would inevitably compel the ZBC to distance their operations from government interference, lest they lose listeners and advertisers to independent and, therefore, more professionally run media outlets. And the appointment of qualified and experienced editors would act as a buffer. ZANU-PF has achieved total control of the media through appointment of unqualified or incompetent, and, therefore, submissive editors.'

In Peta's view, the setting up of private stations should be done through a licensing board divorced from government. 'You need to ensure that licences are not dished out to cronies,' he says, 'so there has to be a transparent authority, appointed by a parliamentary committee and made up of equal representation from any party that has ten or more seats in the House. I think board members should be as independent as judges, maybe not appointed for life but with non-renewable terms of five or seven years, during which they could not be removed except for gross misconduct.'

For Gerry Jackson, who has spent a lifetime in broadcasting, community radio should be a priority:

> Sort out ZBC, make it independent and have lots of diverse programmes with plenty of time for talkback, so that listeners can be part of the mix. When I set up Capital, it wasn't planned as a donor project, so I had to explore the ad market. I worked out that there was enough radio advertising in Zimbabwe for the ZBC and one other commercial venture. But you can have any number of community stations! The equipment is relatively cheap and there could be one in each commuter suburb around Harare – Seke, Mbare, Chitungwiza – and the same in Bulawayo.
>
> Then, as many as you like across the country. The ZBC used to have a wealth of old equipment in the basement. Private media tried to buy it, but were always turned down. Sell this off and get donors and NGOs to fund community studios – we're talking about one room with limited equipment and a small transmitter on the roof – and suddenly, the nation is talking to itself. There would, of course, have to be an independent review body to ensure adherence to basic broadcasting norms and standards and check that there was no hate speech, but there would be no political control over programmes. This truly hands the airwaves back to the people.

But, she adds, no one has done the financial calculations for anything – print or radio – and there's a strong case for donor organisations to draw up blueprints ahead of change so that, come the time, they at least have a shopping list.

While there are many ways to tackle print and radio, television is a different matter. Hugely expensive, setting up a private network from scratch would not be viable. In the late 1990s, the ZBC leased a frequency to an independent station called Joy TV, which quickly out-rated the state channel with new programmes, lively announcers and thirty minutes of news from the BBC. By 2001, in the face of huge public protest, Jonathan Moyo threw the signal off the air, but there is no reason why stations like Joy could not start up again.

Building a society that respects the right to free speech goes beyond the formal media, and requires tolerance from both the government and the public.

In the USA, radical groups like the Black Panthers and the Ku Klux Klan are protected by the First Amendment, which secures their right to make racist and hurtful statements. The laws of libel, slander and a clutch of other legislation allow citizens to sue each other over things that are said, written or publicised, but the state lacks the power to outlaw such statements.

Tricky lines emerge over issues like pornography – worse when it involves rape, bestiality or child abuse – and few would argue against safeguards, but these need to be specific and not open to wide interpretation.

Even in art, freedom can be called to account. In December 2004, a small painting by Chris Savido caused a stir at New York's Chelsea Market. Savido had patched together hundreds of pictures of monkeys and chimpanzees, but, from a distance, the painting bore a likeness to the American president. No accident: it was titled *Bush Monkeys*. Management at the show made him take it down.[4]

Compare that, however, with the experience of Zimbabwean Arnold Buya, 29, who got into an argument with his brother while travelling on a bus in Harare.

'Don't be thick-headed like Mugabe,' he told his brother, only to be arrested by two fellow passengers, who turned out to be plainclothes police. Buya spent Christmas in jail for insulting the president, but his was a light sentence compared with that of Douglas Suangweme, who spent eight months in prison for calling Mugabe a dictator.

Then there's hate speech. Since its inception, the Internet has been used by radical groups that find it hard to get their ideas into the mainstream press. Do a Google search of any linguistic taboo – kaffir, honky, faggot, nigger, slanteyes – and you'll find hundreds, sometimes thousands, of sites. Some are funny and even created by the very groups these words are meant to offend. The gay community has been especially good at this, taking ownership of terms like 'queer' or 'dyke' and neutralising them through common use. In Sydney, there is even a lesbian motorcycle club called Dykes on Bikes.

But there are plenty of sites that summon the faithful to sermons of loathing for blacks, whites, Muslims, Christians, Jews, gays, Americans, Arabs, Indians and Asians. Whoever you are, someone, somewhere hates you.

A few websites get really out of hand, calling for the murder, rape or torture of the targets of their prejudice, and there are those who would argue that the Internet needs some kind of censorship. But who would police such a force, and with what mandate? The very reason that most hate groups build websites is that no one in the mainstream will give them space, because their messages have such narrow appeal. Making cyber-martyrs of these misfits would simply boost their standing, and there is little evidence that their sites produce many converts.

Ironically, it is the seditious and uncontrolled nature of the Internet that has allowed countless political groups to keep in touch on issues of human rights, censorship, torture and bad government. The whistleblower who can't get a hearing can place his or her evidence on the Web and reach the world.

From 1997, Zimbabweans at home and abroad set up more than forty sites, large and small, to pump out news and opinion and maintain the pressure for change, and Mugabe was quick to notice that, for the most part, the Internet was not his ally.

With twelve Internet Service Providers (ISPs) and 100 000

subscribers by 2005, Zimbabwe was Africa's second largest user of the Internet, but Mugabe's attitude was reflected in a speech he made to a UN conference in Rome, when he described the World Wide Web as the tool of 'a few countries in quest of global dominance'. In 2001, a law was passed that allowed the CIO to place filters on any subscriber's account and so obtain copies of their incoming and outgoing e-mails. It also forbade the ISPs from informing clients that their e-mails were being monitored. But in March 2004, the high court ruled the law unconstitutional, so the government tried another route.[5]

In May, it introduced laws making it a crime to use e-mail or the Web for what it called 'anti-national activities'.

The state held a monopoly on regular phone lines that ISPs rely on to reach their clients. Under the new restrictions, ISPs could only use those lines if they agreed to monitor the content of e-mails and report any criticism of the ruling party. One ISP spokesman told a British newspaper: 'It is just not feasible to expect us to look at each and every e-mail message that passes through our system. The volume of traffic makes that impossible. And how would we be able to judge what the government finds objectionable? It would make us the Internet police instead of the Internet providers.'

Zimbabwe's constitution guarantees freedom of expression, but by passing bad laws and stacking the courts, ZANU-PF was able to introduce some of the most odious legislation in the world. Sometimes the courts threw it out, sometimes they didn't. In a future Zimbabwe, freedom will only survive if it is cherished by a government of good faith and a vigilant electorate. But after so many years of oppression, people need to be told about their rights and the importance of protecting these freedoms.

Teaching democracy is like the riddle of which came first, the chicken or the egg. Citizens need to defend themselves against a high-handed state, but only the state can provide the democratic space for such protest. To get a head start, it would make sense for NGOs to begin an awareness campaign among the exiles, who will one day take those skills home with them and teach others about the defence of liberty.

Theatre can be an effective and entertaining way of selling that message, and African writers have long used the stage to lampoon their leaders. In 2004, a Zimbabwean play, *Super Patriots and Morons*, drew crowds in Harare with its witty dialogue about an 'unnamed African country' where people suffer shortages of fuel and food, and the president lives in his own world of privilege, out of touch with those who brought him to power. After twenty performances the play was banned without a reason being given, but the funding of plays with a political edge should be high on the list for donor groups in any new democracy.[6]

In searching for an example of post-liberation success, Iraq would hardly seem a likely candidate. In 2005, bombings and abductions are a daily event, and the scandal of Iraqi prisoners being tortured by US and British troops put an end to hopes that the armies who toppled Saddam Hussein might be viewed as saviours. But the Iraqi media is a different story.

Previously ranked as one of the world's most restrictive press environments, more than 150 new publications, covering a wide range of opinions, have sprung up in the first year of change. Iraqis are now able to gain unfettered access to the Internet and uncensored foreign television broadcasts.[7]

Nevertheless, a continuing lack of security, the murders of at least thirteen journalists, and an ambiguous legal and regulatory media framework remain a problem.

In South Africa, a vibrant civil society has been established since 1994, working with government but maintaining enough distance to allow for independent scrutiny of the state and its agents.

In Zimbabwe, NGOs and human rights groups have also been the victims of legislation banning them from political work, including voter education, and limiting their funds. There has been some effort to develop structures among the exiles so that ready-made groups can be exported back to Zimbabwe when the time is right, but there is neither enough funding nor commitment to make a real difference.

All this work – rebuilding the media and civil society – assumes that Zimbabwe still has enough skilled people to do the job. In my own experience when I was on air at ZBC, by 2000 there was a dearth of technical staff, and the full-time broadcasters were mostly people who could not find work elsewhere and were, therefore, handcuffed to the state, which paid them a small wage in exchange for their loyalty to ZANU-PF. Basildon Peta calls them 'riff-raff who only know how to sing praises for Mugabe'.

Peta, Ncube and Jackson all agree that at least in the short term, foreign skills will be needed to bridge the gap, and, especially, to train local talent in all fields of journalism, technology and media management. In the meantime, millions of Zimbabweans live in exile, many of them unemployed and hungry for education, but little is being done to prepare them for the future.

In the field of broadcasting alone, donors could set up a training studio in Johannesburg and teach exiles from Zimbabwe – and other African countries – the art of radio, creating a skills base for the future. There is no doubt that, come the time, not all graduates will go home, but at least they will have learnt skills to help them gain employment, wherever they decide to live.

But media practitioners make up only one small component of the brain drain that has crippled Zimbabwe, and luring back enough people to rebuild the nation could be the toughest job of all.

6

The Long Way Home

We are starting to feel settled, and I think it would be hard to move everyone back to Zim, even if things came right.

– Ketius Ndhlovu, Zimbabwean exile living in Durban

SOME JOKER, I THINK IT WAS MARK TWAIN, SAID THAT when travelling abroad, people will like you better if you try to speak their language – except for the French, who are determined to hate you anyway.[1] Maybe he wrote this on one of his trips to Africa where, in exchange for a phrase or two, the locals will treat you like family. Black Zimbabweans mostly speak beautiful English, but it's your effort they respect.

So, as you can imagine, speaking Shona, albeit with a lousy accent, made all the difference when I was researching both this book and *The Battle For Zimbabwe*, because people were willing to share with me things they wouldn't normally reveal to strangers, let alone a journalist.

I mention this because you may be surprised at what I'm about to tell you, thinking it at worst a lie, at best, exaggeration: most of the millions of black exiles from Africa who live in Johannesburg have *bought* South African residence permits, birth certificates, passports or asylum papers.

There are no hard figures and I haven't done a survey. If you did ask a polling company to check it out, exiles would probably dodge the issue, fearful of being caught. And if you ask in English, they will tell you they have no documents and live one step ahead of the police. But when I asked the question, more often than not I was shown a genuine South African identity card, listing the holder as having been born in Thohoyandou, Giyani or Durban, the town chosen carefully depending on language.

The Shona and Zulu languages are as different as German and English, but Shonas come from the same ethnic stock as the tiny Venda tribe. The seat of Venda life is Thohoyandou, and this dusty town, less than an hour's drive south of the Limpopo River in South Africa's northernmost province, appears on many birth certificates bought by Zimbabwean exiles. The Shona speakers believe that, if questioned, they might be able to fool a policeman, and this is quite likely true, since most black South Africans can't speak Venda and wouldn't know the difference.

The Shangaans from south-east Zimbabwe favour Giyani near the Kruger National Park as a fake place of origin, because it lies at the heart of South Africa's Shangaan territory. For the Ndebele, anywhere in KwaZulu-Natal will do nicely.

There is nothing empirical about my research, but I have logged more than 800 interviews with black Zimbabweans in South Africa over the past three years, and only a handful had not bought the right to stay. My findings were borne out by research published in March 2005 by the International Organisation for Migration, which conducted a random survey of 500 Zimbabweans living in South Africa. Of those, 68 per cent had documents allowing them to remain in the country.[2] When freedom comes, those exiles with 'legal' status will have a choice: if things look good, they might go home, but they could just as easily stay in South Africa, with its First World comforts.

In Johannesburg, the Department of Home Affairs' old refugee office was in Jorissen Street, near the Nelson Mandela Theatre on the edge of the CBD. On a good day, more than a thousand hopefuls would be lined up around the block, waiting for interviews: people from Cameroon, Kenya, both Congos, Zimbabwe, Mozambique and even the island states of the Seychelles and the Comoros off the east African coast.

To get anywhere near the front of the line, you had to sleep on the pavement overnight, waiting for the doors to open at 8 a.m. But the queue didn't mean much. From sunrise, a dozen or so touts, mostly Nigerian, would move brazenly through the crowd, offering to get people into the building for a fee of R150. This didn't buy you any documents, just an interview. When the office opened, guards would admit perhaps thirty people from the front of the queue, but others would be sneaked in and taken to the desk of a corrupt officer. If you had enough money, your tout could handle everything: leave a set of passport photos and your details and phone number, and he would call when the papers were ready.

One morning, in the company of a few Zimbabwe toughs who had first told me about Jorissen Street, I went there at dawn and watched the circus. When I started taking pictures from across the street, one of the Nigerians walked up to me, bold as brass, and said: 'If you take my photo, I will shoot you dead. Right here!'

My guides, who had been waiting in the shadows, stepped forward and the tout backed off. But there was no doubt that he saw the area as his beat and was not afraid to challenge anyone who threatened the status quo. I carried on taking photographs, but from a distance with a long lens. 'Hill' and 'hero' both start with an 'H', but in my case, that's all they have in common.

Over the next months, I interviewed a number of former Home Affairs employees who were prepared to speak about corruption. They told me about a department in shambles, with passports going for between R2 000 and R15 000, depending on the buyer's nationality.

'It comes down to risk,' one officer explained. 'If it is a South

African who wants to change his or her identity, that's not so expensive. And Zimbabweans too, because they blend in. But if you come from Sudan or Pakistan, it can be harder, because the application stands out in a pile of forms and one of the bosses might ask questions.'

Top price was for Palestinians who wanted South African passports. But the Asians and the Palestinians didn't want to stay. South African passport holders don't need visas to enter Britain, and that was the lure.

In February 2004, in a story for the *Washington Times*, I exposed a racket in which Pakistanis who had been turned down for visas by the South African embassy in Islamabad bought travel documents for Mozambique from that country's honorary consul in Karachi. They then flew to Maputo and travelled by bus into South Africa, bribing the border officials at Komatipoort. Once in Johannesburg, they bought passports and flew to London.

Mozambique moved quickly to end the practice, and, in fairness, the government in Pretoria has done a lot to clean up the mess on their side, but from 1997 until 2004, when the clampdown started, hundreds of thousands – possibly millions – of documents were issued illegally, and all those people now have valid citizen status in South Africa. In 2003, a new director-general, Barry Gilder, took charge at Home Affairs, and promised to put things right. 'Compared with the immigration departments of other countries, ours, to put it bluntly, is a joke,' he told reporters at his first press conference in November that year. Among the problems he had discovered were:

- widespread corruption;
- underpaid officials for whom bribery was a way of supplementing income;
- 1 500 staff vacancies that were placing undue strain on other officials;

- a people-smuggling operation second only to drugs in terms of syndicated crime.

Low wages made staff vulnerable to bribes, and understaffing led to long delays, which prompted clients to offer money in order to speed up legitimate transactions. On top of this there was a huge demand for documents by economic and political refugees who would pay whatever it cost to avoid being deported.

But the numbers from the rest of Africa and the world were small compared with the estimated 3 million Zimbabweans President Thabo Mbeki claimed had entered South Africa. Conventional wisdom has it that when change comes to Zimbabwe, these people will go home. But since so many now have legal status, they will be under no pressure to leave. Corruption has created a new tribe in South Africa, and chances are they are there to stay.

Ketius Ndhlovu, aged thirty-two, made his way to Durban from Bulawayo when the new wave of political violence started in 1999. 'At first it was a temporary move,' he said, 'and for the first six months I sold goods at the side of the road at Umhlanga. At that time I was sharing a shack with five other guys, but then I got a job at a tyre shop. Now my wife is here and our two kids are at primary school, and my wife's brother and my parents will be joining us. We are starting to feel settled, and I think it would be hard to move everyone back to Zim, even if things come right. Maybe when my children have finished their education. For now, I would rather stay here and build a new life with my family.'

Ketius and his wife have both bought South African birth certificates. And, despite the crackdown, when I visited the new refugee office in Rosettenville in April 2005 – Jorissen Street closed down in 2004 – there was little change. The queues were not quite as long, but the touts were there, working the line and taking money in broad daylight. No need for spy cameras or undercover cops to spot the deed – it was happening in full view.

I was also told of a new racket at Johannesburg International Airport, where Pakistanis, fresh off the aeroplane from Karachi and waiting for a connection to Maputo, were being smuggled out of the transit lounge and onto the street through a security entrance.

In 2005, Home Affairs embarked on a new plan to issue tamper-proof 'smart cards' in place of the old ID books, and deputy minister Malusi Gigaba told parliament that the government would produce 'an integrated biometric database of all people: citizens, residents, refugees and illegal foreigners'.

If successful, the card would function as a passport, driving licence, ID book and even a bank card, linked to a national database of fingerprints.[3] But no one had suggested that South African documents were being tampered with – only that they were for sale at the right price – and it is hard to imagine that corrupt officials will not sell the new cards too, though no doubt the price will go up.

South Africa is not the only country with this problem. Prudence is a typical Zimbabwean exile: educated, late twenties and a paid-up member of the Movement for Democratic Change. She had been picked up four times by the police in Bulawayo after attending MDC rallies, and on one of these occasions she was beaten in the cells.

'I needed a new passport,' she told me when we met in the foyer of a posh hotel in Gaborone. 'No one trusts Zimbabweans when they travel. At immigration, they think you're coming there to stay, which many are. So, a year ago, I bought a Botswana passport for 380 Pula ($85).'

The price was more than twice the average monthly wage in Zimbabwe, but, off the record, Botswana officials admit that thousands of passports have been sold by citizens who then report their documents lost, and are given new ones.

'Our old passports are quite easy to fiddle,' one officer told me. 'You can replace the photograph, and we don't have a history of checking up on our own citizens. Now we have made that page tamper-proof, but only on the new-issue documents. There are still plenty of the old ones on sale in Jo'burg and here at home.'

After four years in Gaborone, where she was initially employed as a domestic worker, Prudence is secretary to the chief accountant at the branch office of a South African mining firm, and has learnt to speak Setswana.

'This is my new home,' she said. 'I still love Zimbabwe and my heart is there, but I don't want to leave all that I've worked for here. Even if things come right, I will stay in Botswana.'

For Zimbabweans in Britain, things are different. The Home Office is not easy to bribe, and the new European Union passports are hard to alter. But if necessity is the mother of invention, despair is the father of fraud, and there are plenty of desperate people in Harare. After the MDC lost the 2000 election and voters realised that change might take time, the daily queue for immigration visas grew long at the British and South African embassies.

In 2001, the Southern African Migration Project (SAMP) surveyed 900 Zimbabwe professionals, most of whom were black. Nearly 70 per cent said they were committed to leaving within five years, citing inflation, high tax rates, scarcity of goods, declining salaries, deteriorating medical services and poor prospects for their children.

Statistics are hard to come by, because most people leave illegally, but it is estimated that between 1997 and 2004, around 479 000 Zimbabweans emigrated officially to South Africa, Botswana, Britain and the US. However, unofficial estimates put the number in Britain alone at between 600 000 and 1 million.[4]

Those who could not obtain legal residence abroad went 'on holiday' and stayed, and the number of deportations grew. Immigration officers at London's Heathrow Airport began checking the bags of Zimbabweans, and anyone found with school certificates and an employment résumé was likely to be sent home on the next flight.

It was years since Britain had seen an influx from Africa on this scale. In 1968, Kenya banned dual nationality, and thousands of people with rights to British passports left for London. Four years later, Idi Amin expelled all Asians from Uganda, and 80 000 of them fled to England.[5]

South Africa has long required holiday visas for Zimbabwean travellers, and by 2002 was receiving more than a thousand applications a day, with about the same number moving illegally across the length of the 200-kilometre border between the two countries.[6] For a fee, a small army of guides lead the *girigamba*, or 'dung beetles', across the Limpopo. *Girigamba* is not an insult, but refers to the fact that those leaving their homeland for good carry all their possessions in a bundle, like the beetle heaving his ball of dung.

In 2002, Britain and other EU countries imposed a visa regime, and applicants had to show bank statements, employment records and other evidence that they were not cutting links with home. Rackets sprang up at several embassies in Harare, with bribes being paid just to get an interview. Police officers monitoring the queues acted as middlemen, taking kickbacks for visa officers. People who paid received faster service; those who didn't could wait for days, and then have their applications denied.

In 2004, the going price for help in acquiring a South African visa was $180, while the cost of a British document was close on $1 000. Diplomats denied the story, but in January 2004, twelve police and five army officers were arrested after police conducted a raid at the British Embassy in an effort to curb the scam.[7]

Whereas the South Africans had been grudgingly tolerant of immigration, in Britain it was becoming an election issue. And it wasn't just Zimbabweans they resented. The British perception was that people from Africa, India, Pakistan, Sri Lanka, Turkey and Eastern Europe were pouring into their country, and that controls imposed by Tony Blair's Labour government were so weak, they actually made London a target for those in search of a better life.

A UK opinion poll published in December 2004 showed that a record level of immigration was the principal concern of voters, ahead of health, education, crime and terrorism. Nearly three quarters of respondents believed that the system was out of control, and 86 per cent thought that Britain was being 'overrun with asylum seekers'. Even groups normally regarded as liberal, including Londoners and the young, were ill-disposed towards migrants. Home secretary David Blunkett, who resigned at the end of 2004, had not helped by saying that when it came to the number of people Britain could accommodate, he saw 'no obvious limit'.[8]

Day after day, the press exposed stories that helped to harden attitudes. Immigration was at a record high, with a nett average growth of around 170 000 people a year, and Home Office incompetence had allowed in thousands who would otherwise have been denied entry.[9]

The opposition Conservative Party claimed that the average British household was paying up to £160 in a tax year to cover the cost of bogus asylum seekers.[10] Clearing the backlog of appeals and applications would cost an estimated £500 million,[11] but, in addition, 66 per cent of AIDS sufferers in Britain come from countries like Zimbabwe, and treating them was costing another £200 million a year.[12]

The litany of social problems linked to immigration went on and on. A rise in crime was linked to gangs whose members were new immigrants unable to find work;[13] identity fraud involving credit cards, passports and social welfare was growing at 165 per cent a year and costing Britain £1.3 billion annually, with much of the crime blamed on migrants;[14] figures tabled in parliament showed that 2 000 people a month were being smuggled across the English Channel in the back of freight trucks, right under the nose of the Customs Service;[15] and even Blair conceded that, on the matter of Africa, 'we must now all accept the utter futility of trying to shut our borders'.[16]

Opposition leader Michael Howard turned up the heat: 'I'd like to say to the United Nations High Commissioner for Refugees, we will take 15 000 people a year, people we know are all genuine refugees,' he told voters. 'Then we really would be giving sanctuary to those who are fleeing persecution and torture and not those who simply have enough money to pay the people smugglers.'[17]

In the 1960s, when Enoch Powell predicted that wide-scale migration from South Asia would lead to 'rivers of blood', others claimed that the new workers were doing unskilled jobs that Brits had grown out of. In post-war England everyone had an education, and councils were struggling to recruit gardeners, labourers and grave diggers.

But by 2000 Britain had become mechanised, and lower-level white-collar work, like answering the phone at a call centre, had been outsourced to Asia. In January 2005, Howard sounded a new warning: 'Britain has reached a turning point,' he said. 'Our communities cannot absorb newcomers at today's pace. Immigration must be brought under control. It is essential for good community relations, national security and the management of public services.'[18]

And right near the top of the list of 'newcomers,' were

Zimbabweans. Asylum applications were dominated by three countries: Iraq, Zimbabwe and Somalia, but on average nine out of ten requests were turned down, after which there was a drawn-out process of appeal before deportation. In 2002, Britain adopted a policy of 'non-return' for Zimbabweans, which meant that, if you could get in, by whatever means, you could stay. The result was a free-for-all.

Late in 2003, Mucheri Moyo crossed the Limpopo, bought a South African passport in the name of Elvis Sipho Malope, and flew to London. There he told authorities that he was fleeing oppression back home, but was arrested and deported to Johannesburg, where police met him at the airport and took him to the Lindela deportation camp at Krugersdorp. But friends in London used the 'non-return' policy to challenge the Home Office, and won. The British government had to pay Mucheri's fare back to London, where he was granted leave to stay.

A favourite ploy was to enrol at a college and then apply for extensions, long after the course had finished. Only 790 UK student visas were issued in Zimbabwe during 2003, and 2 850 nationals were logged as studying in Britain, yet 10 535 extensions were granted.

But for some, the only way through the red tape was with money. An undercover investigation in June 2004 exposed the sale of fake asylum papers by a Zimbabwean couple based in Birmingham. For £1 000, the client was given a national insurance number and a letter from the Home Office granting leave to stay.

Another bust by police in London and their South African counterparts in Durban netted a Zimbabwean syndicate selling enrolment letters to non-existent colleges. The culprits had allegedly earned more than a million pounds in the space of three years selling the letters, visa stamps and even passports.[19]

Now ask yourself: If Zimbabweans have gone to such lengths to enter Britain and stay there, battling racism, bureaucracy, a hostile press and public outrage; if, despite all this, they still clamour to get in, waiting up to five years for legal residency, how likely are they, when change comes, to give up all they have won and go home?

Kanna Chisango, who left Zimbabwe in 2000 and now works at a private hospital in Manchester, believes this simply will not happen. 'It took so long to get residence here,' she told me, 'and to bring my husband and my parents across, that I can't see myself going back. I earned nothing as a senior nursing sister in Harare, and even in Britain the pay is not that good, but we have established ourselves. We still have a house in Harare that is rented out and we go back as often as we can to see family, but next year I hope to get a British passport, and this is becoming home to me. My twins will start school here in 2006 – they're already in kindergarten – and I think they have a better future in Manchester than in a new Zimbabwe. It hurts me to say that, but it's how I feel. And I have no doubt that most here will stay. We've paid a high price in pain and time to win a place here.'

In public, most say they will return as soon as they can, but if you push, the answers become blurred. Some will wait and see, others would need a guaranteed job back home. Few say they'll be on the first flight out of Heathrow.

For Jack Sithole, late of Chipinge and now writing credit-card software in Cardiff, it's lifestyle that will keep him in Britain: 'The phones work, broadband runs the Net, trains run on time, and you can spend your money on anything you can afford without having to queue or buy on the black market. I would find it hard to adjust back home. I miss the sunshine, but when I visit now, I find Zimbabwe very slow. Here we have e-commerce over the Net; there you hardly have an economy. I'm not even sure I'd find something good in my line.'

In Britain, virtual shopping notched up £6.4 billion in 2004, and is expected to reach £19 billion by the end of the decade, much of it on groceries delivered to the door.[20] Zimbabwe has not even progressed to paying by credit card over the phone or by e-mail (the signatory must be present in person).

But the convenience of Britain, with 160 million plastic cards in circulation, adds to the stress levels that put Western countries way ahead of Africa when it comes to strokes, heart disease, cancer and nervous breakdowns.

In 2005, UK credit card debt reached an all-time high of £55 billion,[21] and the pressure of both partners working, the high cost of child care, traffic jams and little family support rated high among Zimbabwean exiles airing thoughts of going home.

Fiona Garwe, who works as a London travel agent, misses the easy pace of Harare: 'Families there help one another. You always have aunts, sisters, cousins ready to help with the children, and weekends are times to chill. Here, I work six days a week and my husband is in Germany, cleaning factories. My daughter Victoria is eight now, and she spends her time at school and in day care. I would rather take my chances at home, but not as things are now. If change comes, I will be gone. Here I'm becoming a stranger to myself.'

And, she concedes, there are other issues. 'I'm not sure I want Vicky to grow up here. We can't afford a private school, and the education at government schools is not so good. Also, when I look at teenage British kids, I don't want my daughter to become like that. No respect, no manners.'

Fiona's concern is not unique. Many Zimbabweans I spoke to coach their children in the evenings to make up for what they feel is inadequate schooling in the public system. This is borne out by several British social workers, migration consultants, Home Office workers and teachers, who told me that migrants from Zimbabwe, South Africa, Zambia, Kenya, Ghana and Uganda arrive in Britain more literate and numerate – and therefore more employable – than many local school-leavers.

The British army has long been used as a research tool to test the ability of school-leavers who do not intend going on to college. At the entry level of private soldier, recruits come from a wide cross-section of geographic and social backgrounds, and are representative of youngsters who might otherwise join the trades or become semi-skilled workers. According to the army, they must have skills 'widely accepted as the minimum level required to work and function in society in general'.

But a 2004 study of more than 2 000 young adults, who applied to join the ranks in the previous year, showed that half the candidates had the reading and writing skills of eleven-year-olds, while 20 per cent were at the level of seven-year-old children.[22]

Whether or not people want to return, Zimbabwe is in desperate need of talent. One study suggests that nine out of ten university graduates have left, and recruitment firms complain that they cannot fill their clients' needs because there are simply no people to do the jobs. In Pretoria, Gabriel Shumba has set up the Zimbabwe Exiles' Forum (ZEF), a database of names, skills and locations. 'It is not in any way political,' he says. 'This is a system for the future so that, when things change and we need bankers, nurses, farmers, teachers, accountants, vets or whatever, at least we'll know where to find them. Whether they want to come home is up to them, but at least they can be offered jobs when the economy opens up.'

Gabriel started ZEF in 2003, but it took him eighteen months to get a small amount of funding. 'Everyone said what a great idea it was,' he told me, 'but I don't think that NGOs and the donor community realise the size of the task ahead. They think it can be fixed when change comes, instead of using the downtime we have now to get things moving. I'm not sure anyone understands the scale of the problem. Getting our people home is going to be a task without parallel in the history of southern Africa.'

But many of the exiles who do choose to return could find themselves locked out. In the late 1980s, Zimbabwe changed the law on dual nationality inherited from Rhodesia, and those with two passports had to choose. Retaining your foreign passport – mostly British, South African, Greek, Portuguese or Indian – did not mean leaving the country; you lost your Zimbabwe citizenship, but were granted permanent residence.

Then, ahead of the 2002 election, Mugabe changed the law again, so that only those born of parents who were both Zimbabweans were deemed to be true nationals. Others had to formally renounce their current and future rights to foreign citizenship and produce proof that they had done so, or lose their existing status.

The intention was to disenfranchise voters of European or regional descent, including the sons and daughters of migrants from Zambia and Malawi, who had come to Rhodesia when it was still part of the Central African Federation, because they were inclined to support the MDC. A Zimbabwean found with a foreign passport could be stripped of his or her nationality and deported.

With so many exiles having bought or legally acquired British, Botswana or South African citizenship, Mugabe's law could be a disincentive to going back. A survey of Zimbabwean exiles in the UK and South Africa found that 42 per cent felt they could not contribute to Zimbabwe's future development unless they were allowed to hold more than one passport.[23] Rwanda and South Africa have both passed laws allowing dual nationality in an effort to woo their people home, and Zimbabwe could change the law, but some, like Tawanda Chinoshava from Buhera, now working north of Pretoria, have concerns: 'It can be a good plan, but what about the criminal gangs who slip from country to country? They will use the system to commit crimes in Zimbabwe, and then move in and out on different passports so they can't be caught at the borders. It needs some thought.'

In Uganda, where there is a strong lobby for dual citizenship, the debate was dominated by paranoia, with critics citing a lack of patriotism, divided loyalty and outright danger to the country in times of war when these fence-sitters might side with the enemy. Even so, in 2005 Uganda is moving towards acceptance that, before its millions of foreign-based nationals can be drawn home, they will have to be allowed to retain citizenship of both their adopted country and the land of their birth.[24]

But what of the wretched and destitute living in squatter camps around Johannesburg? Will they go home because, no matter how hard, life in a free Zimbabwe would be an improvement on their current lot?

Since I began doing research among Zimbabwean exiles in June 2002, the concentration of down-and-outs has shrunk noticeably. That's not to say everyone is doing well, but not as many seem to be roughing it. They have found jobs, joined up with friends to share the rent on better accommodation, and started carving out a future. Even so, from my discussions in Hillbrow, Yeoville and the slums of Johannesburg and Durban, the hard-up individuals are more likely to return than those who have done well.

Ironically, those who are worst off can be found in Botswana, which has one of Africa's most thriving economies. Outside the beer halls in Gaborone, Zimbabwean girls, some well below the age of consent, sell themselves late at night when patrons stumble out in drunken lust. During the day, young men – mostly from Bulawayo because of its proximity to the Botswana border – stand in groups near the CBD, waiting to be picked up for short-term building work.

No asylum papers here. The police don't take bribes, and

exiles have to live by their wits. By February 2005, an estimated 2 500 were being deported every month at a cost of $15 000 to the Botswana government.

When I passed through Gaborone in September 2004, those who had not bought passports told me they wanted to leave, but not for home. Instead, they planned to push on to Johannesburg.

If my hunch proves correct, a large number of exiles, especially skilled people who have been successful abroad, will stay where they are. But it doesn't have to be that way. In Afghanistan, a Return for Qualified Afghans programme (RQA) is being run by the international Organisation for Migration, co-funded by the EU. Comprehensive assistance packages are offered to qualified Afghans now living in Europe who wish to work in the public and private sector, including:

- firms providing goods for the domestic market;
- civil and social services;
- public infrastructure;
- rural development.

Candidates apply to a programme officer, who checks their qualifications against a list of vacancies in Kabul and other centres. Once a match is made and the employer approves the application, money is provided for travel and relocation costs. Since the selection of candidates is based on employer needs, it's a three-way win result for the exile, the firm and Afghanistan.

A self-employment option offers grants of up to €5 000 per person for those wishing to start their own small businesses; women are encouraged to apply and receive an extra monthly allowance.

Along with the US, Britain will be a major donor when it comes to funding Zimbabwe's recovery, but would London back a plan to send people home? Perhaps not in all fields. There are so many Zimbabwean nurses in Britain that any programme to encourage their return could leave a hole in the UK health system.

In London, the Royal College of Nursing spoke of a crisis in the profession as British nurses moved to better-paid jobs. An ageing workforce and the growing number of qualified staff being lured to other English-speaking countries, especially America, were also undermining the health system. Dr Beverly Malone, the college's general secretary, warned that 'the foundations of nursing are built on sand, not stone'. Holding the system together, she said, were health workers from other countries.

Between 1994 and 2003, the number of registrations by foreign-trained nurses increased from 11 to 43 per cent of the total, and Zimbabweans were near the top of the list.[25] This raises the question of whether Britain would encourage nurses to leave England, let alone pay for them to go.

Among those of all colours, vocations and social calling – especially the young – there will be some who feel the urge to return simply for the chance to experience freedom on their own soil. The feel-good factor saw a short-term repatriation to many Eastern European countries after the fall of communism and to South Africa in 1994, but the euphoria soon ebbed, and the flow dried up and then reversed.

Given that millions have left Zimbabwe, even a small percentage of returnees would number tens of thousands, and their sudden arrival might not be good news for those who have stayed. The cost of rent, especially in the townships, will skyrocket as the newcomers arrive with their rands, able to pay a premium price for accommodation, and this could lead to ill feeling and even conflict within communities.

Planning for the inflow will be important, and temporary

homes should be erected near the cities where squatter camps may otherwise spring up. Power and sanitation will be needed, and there will be pressure on the public transport system, which will most likely be quick to raise fares. Goods in shops and on the black market will jump in price if thousands of new consumers enter the fray, and whoever is in government will need strategies to avoid a social meltdown.

A smooth transition will take planning, yet nothing has been done on this front, and no one is talking money or budgets, hoping, it seems, that 'it will all be all right on the night'. But, in addition to the urge to celebrate change, there's another emotion that may kick in: revenge. In Britain and South Africa, there are many who say they are waiting to 'sort out the past'.

Simon, aged thirty-two, and his brother Pybus, aged twenty-seven, come from a small village south of Hwange National Park in Matabeleland, and have been in Johannesburg since 2001. Simon's story appeared as one of four torture testimonies in *The Battle for Zimbabwe*, and is repeated here only because it relates to a key issue on the future relationship between political exiles and those who forced them to flee.

> At the end of August 2002, I was picked up by war vets and militia in Bulawayo, because I was working in the MDC security department. They took me first to an empty farmhouse outside Bulawayo and beat me, asking for details of the next MDC meeting, our campaigns and whether we had any guns. I told them some things, which they already knew, but said I had never seen any guns and they beat me more with a sjambok [leather whip]. I was still wearing my clothes, but was handcuffed with my hands behind me. This was around four in the afternoon.
>
> At about 7 o'clock that night, I was led to a truck and they pushed me into the back of the pick-up. We drove to Nkayi outside Bulawayo, to another empty farm at a place

I did not know. When I got out of the truck, they removed my shoes and my long trousers but left me with my shorts and T-shirt. I was taken to an area of trees and made to sit on the ground. They told me they were waiting for their leader, a war vet called [name supplied] to arrive.

About an hour passed, then I was told that the man had arrived, and someone put a blindfold over my eyes and led me into a farm building. They undid the handcuffs, removed all my clothes and lay me on the floor on my stomach. Then one of the war vets started to beat me on my buttocks with a sjambok, asking again about guns.

When he had finished, I was told to sit up and open my mouth, because they were going to urinate into it. I did as I was told and felt someone's penis on my lips and the hot urine squirted into my mouth. I spat it out and was pushed to the ground and beaten again with the sjambok. They sat me up again and told me they would repeat the exercise and, again, a man put his penis into my mouth and urinated and I swallowed it. They told me to keep my mouth open and now an erect penis was placed on my lips and I could feel the pulse of a man masturbating himself. I heard him grunting and his semen flowed into my mouth.

I choked as it went down my throat and I vomited, and they shouted and swore at me and pulled me to the ground again and beat my buttocks with the sjambok. Then the process was repeated with several men, some with urine, some with semen, and I swallowed it all.

When they finally released me, they removed the blindfold and I saw the people who tortured me.

My problem is that, a few days later, my gums started bleeding and this still happens. My brain is still heavy and crying with the experience and, although my wife is here now, we have not had sex since that time when I was abducted.

I left Zimbabwe, but the CIO visited my parents at their rural home and beat both my mother and father, asking

> for my whereabouts. Then they took my father outside and beat him separately while they kicked and beat my mother inside the hut. She later died of her injuries and I was not able to go home for her funeral.
>
> I need to see a doctor to talk about my problems and also to check my mouth. But there are horrible things in my brain when I think about what has happened to me. Really, I just want to die sometimes. It is so terrible.

I had done this interview in January 2003. More than two years later, I interviewed the brothers again, this time about going home. I wanted to know the first things they would do in Zimbabwe, and expected to hear talk of family reunions and cattle, catching up with friends and looking for work.

'I want to find the men who killed my mother and I want to torture them to death,' Simon said without hesitation.

I don't know why, but my first impulse was to laugh. I didn't, and there was silence until Pybus said: 'They must pay with their cries.'

'You can't do that,' I said, and was about to explain the principles of court justice, but Simon cut me short. 'Yes, I can,' he said. Silence again.

'What about the people who tortured you?' I asked.

'I will beat them. I can take my revenge and they will understand. But my mother was innocent. She had done nothing, she was not involved in politics. There was no excuse.'

The brothers' urge to exact revenge prompted me to question others among the more than 100 torture victims I had interviewed. Sure enough, most spoke not of jail or justice, but personal vendetta.

Nkathazo Ncube was captured by the youth brigade in 2002. After beating him at their camp, they crushed his testicles, causing permanent injury. In Johannesburg, Dr Len Weinstein, who has helped dozens of torture victims at my behest and without charge, treated Nkathazo for depression and referred him to an urologist, Dr Stephen Cornish, who was able to repair the damage in February 2005.

'I am so grateful that people have put things right,' Nkathazo told me after the operation. 'Now all that is left is to punish the ones who did this. I have their names and I will not stop until my work is done.'

Among those I interviewed, women who had been raped and beaten felt inclined to rely on the courts, but their husbands wanted vengeance. However, most of the Matabele who had lost families two decades earlier in *Gukurahundi* opted for a judicial commission to put the killers on trial, rather than settling old scores themselves.

If I had the proverbial dollar for every time some analyst told me that Zimbabwe would end in civil war, I could start a pension fund, but those who know the country and its people don't see that as a realistic outcome, no matter what happens.

Vigilante killings are a different matter. In the new housing estates built for returnees, hundreds of young men fresh from exile, hard of heart and without work to fill their days, could unleash a new terror. If only one per cent of the tens of thousands of victims and their families see this through, the return of exiles could be a bloody affair, not on a scale that would destroy the country, but serious enough to derail the programmes needed to attract investment and rebuild society.

Gukurahundi was based, in part, on a desire by the Shona to pay back the Matabele for the massacres they had suffered under Lobengula and Mzilikazi a hundred years before, and neither Africa nor the world saw it coming.

In planning a role for the scatterlings of Zimbabwe's diaspora, those who map out the country's future will have to take account of the suffering to which so many have been subjected, and build in a programme for swift and visible justice.

7

I Was Only Following Orders

Military law has long recognised that following orders is a legitimate defence, but not if an order was illegal or if a person of ordinary sense and understanding would have known it was illegal.

– Pete Williams, NBC News, 6 May 2004, commenting on the trial of US soldiers charged with abusing Iraqi prisoners at Abu Ghraib

THE WORST MASS MURDERERS OF RECENT TIMES HAVE gone unpunished, and the guilty walk among us. After World War II, the Nazi elite were tried at Nüremberg, and a limited number of Japanese war criminals faced the same fate in Tokyo. Some were executed, others jailed, but tragically the world paid no attention to the same crimes committed on a larger scale in Russia and China.

If you believe Russian author and Nobel Prize winner Alexander Solzhenitsyn, an estimated 66.7 million people died under the repressive regimes of Lenin, Stalin and Khruschev between 1917 and 1959.

As for China, the *Guinness Book of Records* estimates that in just three years, from 1966 to 1969, 63.7 million Chinese perished in the so-called Cultural Revolution.[1]

The perpetrators were never pursued, and whereas Europe, Australia and the US have laws that allow Nazi war criminals to be arrested more than sixty years after the fact, the same rules don't apply to the Soviet and Chinese killers ... or those who served under Pol Pot in Cambodia or Idi Amin in Uganda.

But that was in the bad old days. Those responsible for more recent massacres in East Timor, Rwanda, Sierra Leone, Iraq and the former Yugoslavia *have* been put on trial; some have already been jailed and, in this new millennium, the world has become a dangerous place for tyrants.

As a condition of stepping down, some rulers were granted immunity from prosecution, and in Zimbabwe the question of a pardon for Mugabe is said to have scuppered talks between ZANU-PF and the MDC.

But amnesties don't always work, as in the case of General Augusto Pinochet of Chile, who led a coup against the democratically elected government of Salvador Allende in 1973. Pinochet's regime was marked by death and torture, and he only retired in 1990 in exchange for lifelong immunity. But on a visit to London in 1998 he was arrested on a Spanish warrant, and would have been tried in Madrid had he not been sent home by the British government on grounds that he was too ill to stand trial.

As democracy became entrenched in Santiago, there were calls for the former president to be tried in Chile, but the problems were twofold: he still had immunity, and doctors claimed that he had lost his mind. Then, in November 2003, he made the mistake of granting an interview to a Miami television station, and appeared quite lucid as he defended his record. In 2004, the United States Congress reported that, far from being senile as his doctors had claimed, Pinochet was communicating with Riggs Bank in Washington, where he had stashed up to $8 million of looted cash.

Not only did this demonstrate his mental acuity, it also shocked his supporters, who had defended the general's carefully cultivated reputation as an austere leader who brooked no corruption. At the end of August 2004, Chile's Supreme Court lifted the immunity order and declared the eighty-eight-year-old general competent to stand trial.[2]

In spite of loopholes that allowed so many killers to go free, Nüremberg, Yugoslavia, Rwanda, Sierra Leone, the Truth and Reconciliation Commission (TRC) in South Africa, and the ruling in Santiago each created, layer by layer, a series of precedents that made it easier to put other leaders and their lieutenants on trial once they left office.

Among the Zimbabwean exiles in Johannesburg, I am in touch with what I call a 'Survivors' Circle', a group of people who have suffered and survived, though not unscathed. At its height in 2003, there were forty-four souls in the circle, and I tried to meet with each of them at least once a month.

After my first book was published, I spent more and more time outside South Africa, giving talks around the world, never turning down an invitation if it offered the chance to explain what was happening in Zimbabwe.

In speech and writing I steer away from adjectives, because their meaning can be misinterpreted. Talk about 'a big house', and someone who lives in one room may see it as a mansion. But, if you already own a mansion, your notion of a big house might be different and, in the same way, what people understand by *evil* acts or *gross* abuse can be relative. So, instead I let the stories speak for themselves, retelling what I've heard in the circle.

There's Spooky, aged twenty-seven, from Masvingo, who suffered permanent lung damage when he was repeatedly drowned and resuscitated during interrogation by the CIO. He was held down and forced to swallow water poured through a funnel placed in his mouth. When his stomach distended, his captors would jump on him, but as the bloody mixture came spewing back, he wasn't allowed to sit up and clear his mouth before the next jug of water was poured down his throat. Next, they used burning rolls of newspaper to 'shave' the hair from his chest and groin.

Grover, twenty-two, from Mutare can't hear properly, because his eardrums were punctured with a screwdriver. Teresa of Gokwe walks with a limp after her feet were burnt; Florens from Buffalo Range was hit so hard in the lower spine that her vertebrae are out of alignment; and when Brian from Karoyi takes off his shirt, you can see where the war veterans used a knife to carve the letters MDC on his back.

But there are also tales to warm your heart. In November 2002, Spooky's brother, Givemore, was raped by the youth militia, just one of some forty-two cases of male rape that came to my attention. Givemore's wife, Sipho, suffered the same punishment at the hands of war veterans – she wasn't sure how many – over a period of three days.

In Johannesburg two months later, separately and in confidence, they told me the stories that they had not yet been able to tell each other. Rape carries a stigma in all societies, and hugely so in black culture. Both Givemore and Sipho said they had problems with intimacy, were uncomfortable with being touched and revolted by the thought of sex. Initially, they were treated by Dr Len Weinstein, who has specialised in the treatment of mental and physical trauma for nearly forty years.

At my request – and without charge – Len has worked with countless torture victims, both to verify their stories through medical examinations and to heal their wounds. Despite having a busy practice in the wealthy Johannesburg suburb of Sandton, he and his colleague, Dr Junaid Hoosen, and their staff, Di, Rachel and Celia, always make time for members of the circle.

Len prescribed anti-depressants for Givemore and Sipho, after which they went for counselling at the Centre for the Study of Violence and Reconciliation in Braamfontein, an NGO staffed by mental health workers who, at no cost to the patient, help victims to cope with the horror.

For more than a year, the couple lived together without any change. Then, in the wake of a row about something trivial, they both broke down and told their stories ... and made love. In November 2004, Sipho gave birth to a son, and shortly after Christmas they came to show me their baby. Givemore was working as a clerk, Sipho's mother had arrived from Masvingo to help with the child, and from the smiles and animated conversation, they had clearly moved on and were starting to build a new life.

But what about the life they'd lost, the pain, the eighteen months of anguish, the need to flee their home? Does all that have a price? And, if so, who should pay? Not just for Givemore and Sipho, but for Grover, Teresa, Florens, Brian and thousands of others who have been tortured by agents of the state or had their homes burnt down, relatives killed and lives destroyed, not least among them the victims of *Gukurahundi.*

When I speak in Washington, London, Sydney or Johannesburg, I always raise the issue of justice and invite the audience to share their views. Some push for war crimes trials, others for a South African-style TRC, and a minority hold the equally valid view that a new government needs to draw a line and move on, because dragging up the past will only hold back the future and delay the healing that is so vital to national progress.

But the circle is of one mind: all want justice, and would be willing to aid the process by testifying against their tormentors, though some of the rape victims say they would prefer to make their statements in camera.

A frightening number, all men, are set to take revenge unless – and, in a few cases, even *if* – the state is willing to act not just against those who committed the outrage, but also the officers and ministers, and even the president, who sanctioned it – or, at best, did nothing to halt the madness.

So where, you may ask, is the problem? Hold some trials, punish the guilty, free the innocent or those whose cases don't stack up, and move on. But life is rarely that simple, and there are many legal, moral and practical issues that need to be considered:

- Does what had happened in a sovereign state, such as in Zimbabwe, qualify under the accepted definition of 'crimes against humanity'?
- When would the trials or truth commission take place? Arrests too soon after democratic change could spark a coup by security force officers fearing prosecution. Perhaps an amnesty would be better.
- What time frame would be covered? From 2000? Everything since 1980? The civil war in the 1970s? Political detentions from 1965?
- Should amnesty be granted to those willing to testify against their comrades?
- Who would decide guilt or innocence – judges, a jury, or special commissioners? And in the case of the last two, how would you select a panel that wasn't loaded in favour of one side?
- What steps could be taken to minimise personal acts of revenge?
- Would it be physically possible to try tens of thousands of suspects, or should only those involved in the most serious crimes be brought to book?
- What of those who skipped the country? Should international warrants be issued? In London, the Pinochet case showed how lengthy and expensive this could be, when his appeal against extradition to Spain dragged on for seventeen months.

- On the subject of appeals, should those found guilty be free to contest the verdict?
- Should the defence, 'I was only following orders' be accepted, and, if so, on what grounds?
- Who would pay for research, translation, arrest, detention and the assembling of witnesses, and the recruitment of a tribunal, secretaries, typists and a legion of defence lawyers to represent each of the accused? And if victims are to be compensated, who pays for that?
- Finally, would a future government be willing to make the process all-inclusive? Victor's justice can spark new resentment, so those in the MDC who have killed members of ZANU-PF – or murdered CIO officers spying on exiles in Johannesburg – would also need to be tried or brought before the commission.

If the task sounds daunting, that's because it is. Just look at other countries where courts are in session. Nearly ten years after the war in Yugoslavia, Slobodan Milosevic is still on trial, and major war criminals like Radovan Karadzic and Ratko Mladic – linked to the murder in 1995 of more than 7 000 Bosnian Muslims in Srebrenica – remain at large.[3]

In Rwanda, 100 000 suspects in the 1994 genocide waited a decade before being tried. During that time, they were held in overcrowded jails and without proper food or sanitation.[4]

The special court in Sierra Leone, set up in partnership with the UN to try some of the worst crimes in African history, was hampered by a lack of funds.[5]

The principles are easy. International treaties on crimes against humanity make clear that torture, forced exile, political murder and genocide are matters for global justice, and in theory, perpetrators can be arrested anywhere in the world, even if they have left the country where the offence took place.

And because these crimes are, by definition, universal, amnesties don't count because they only apply to the country that granted them. When Pinochet was arrested in London, he had full immunity back home, but it carried no weight outside Chile. Some scholars even hold that amnesties are illegal because they conflict with the international obligation of *all* countries – including the one granting the amnesty – to apprehend those charged with war crimes.[6]

I don't want to lose your attention by getting bogged down in legal jargon, but if you do a Google search, you'll find hundreds of sites listing laws and well-accepted precedents that more than cover the case of Zimbabwe. So, what about the time frame? How far back should we go in our hunt for suspects?

In August 2003, a symposium in Johannesburg on the possibility of war crimes trials in Zimbabwe brought together a wide range of human rights groups, and the London-based Redress Trust produced a booklet on their findings. Redress is an international NGO that seeks justice for the victims of torture.

The Johannesburg forum called for a wide-ranging inquiry dating back to white settlement in 1890, but some argued that the cost would be prohibitive. One solution would be to focus on *Gukurahundi* and more recent violence, because there is plenty of evidence and the loss suffered by victims is still current. Another, smaller, commission could look at other periods of violence. This shouldn't be seen as reducing the seriousness of crimes committed in different eras, but an all-or-nothing approach could see the whole project derailed by cost.

Commissioners for both panels could be drawn from human rights groups, the law, religion, trade unions, universities and NGOs. Other aspects like appeal, witness protection and the sheer magnitude of the scheme await the attention of a new government, which will have plenty of models to draw on.

And an extensive public relations campaign will be needed

to convince victims that justice is coming and to warn against acts of retribution. Those brought before the courts with formal cases to answer will need state-funded lawyers to plead their defence, or a new government could be accused of staging show trials.

But how do you defend such gruesome acts of murder, torture and destruction? One plea will almost certainly be the Nüremberg defence, named for its frequent use during the Nazi trials in 1946: 'I was only following orders.'

It was first offered by Rudolf Hoess, commandant of the Auschwitz death camp and later grand overlord of the extermination process in which 6 million Jews, gypsies and homosexuals were killed between 1940 and 1945. At his trial, Hoess, then forty-six, insisted that he had grown up in a society where orders were sacrosanct, and could not have been expected to challenge the system. He was hanged at Auschwitz on 16 April 1947.[7]

Soldiers, lawyers and academics reviewed this defence after it cropped up in 2004 at the trial of Americans charged with abusing inmates at the Abu Ghraib prison near Baghdad after the second Iraqi war. One of the accused, Sergeant Ivan 'Chip' Frederick, had even checked the procedure at Abu Ghraib. 'He did attempt to find out if what he was doing was correct, and he was told that it was,' Frederick's lawyer, Gary Myers, told the court martial.[8] Military law requires all ranks to follow any legal order from a senior officer and, if in doubt, the fallback is to ask for the order in writing. But it can be hard for young soldiers to judge what is right, especially in wartime.

For example, were the 1 200 Allied pilots who carried out the fire-bombing of Dresden on 13 February 1945 committing a legal act? The town was not a military target and was packed with German civilians trying to escape the Russian army that was advancing from the east. More than 25 000 women and children died in the flames and, although no one was ever charged with commanding the raid, at the 60th commemoration in 2005, several scholars described it as a war crime.[9]

These days it is widely accepted that, within reason, a person in armed service may ask to be excused from taking part in any given action on grounds of conscience. But in Zimbabwe, it would be hard for a soldier or policeman to challenge an order without the risk of punishment, and, in the youth brigade, those who step out of line are beaten, tortured or even raped. For this reason, a claim of following orders – where proven – would have to be taken into account, not in determining guilt but in passing sentence, and not in the case of senior officers or government ministers, who were running the show.

For those pressed into service as agents of ZANU-PF at local level, either because they were caught up in the frenzy of the moment or too scared to refuse, there's the problem of making peace with their communities. Bringing these people before a court or TRC on charges of arson, violence and pillage might not be the most efficient or effective way of doing business, and could still leave the accused at odds with the victims and their families, slowing down the process of reconciliation.

In Rwanda, the new government set up hundreds of *gaçaca* (pronounced gachacha) courts, at which a community hears both the victims and the wrongdoers, and passes sentence. More often than not, the procedure mends relations between the two. It's a slow process, but faster than dragging thousands of bit players before a central body, such as a court or commission.

Gaçaca means 'grass', and the name comes from the fact that the hearings usually take place on the lawn in the local town square. These are no kangaroo courts, but real and compassionate places of healing. The accused may still be living in the village, or could just as easily be in jail awaiting trial.

Those who act as judges receive training at government level, and the court can pass sentence, including jail, but the concept is more about forcing perpetrators to look their victims in the eye and display true sorrow and remorse for what they have done, and to beg forgiveness for their acts of madness, carried out at the behest of the former government. It is a model that could be adapted by Zimbabwe, but only at village level. For those guilty of murder and mass torture, especially at senior level, community courts, like amnesties, can breed a culture of impunity and do little to satisfy victims' need for satisfaction.

Gaçaca courts are a lot cheaper than the real thing, but there are many of them, so the costs accumulate. Add this to the price tag of a TRC and war crimes trials, and you arrive back at one of the major hurdles: who is going to pay?

In its first five years, the International Criminal Tribunal for Rwanda (ICTR), which tried the most serious cases at a special court in Arusha in neighbouring Tanzania, spent close to $1 billion and secured less than thirty convictions.

Agencies of the UN work in mysterious ways and are notoriously expensive. South Africa's TRC cost just over $30 million and covered a much wider gamut, examining events from 1960 to 1994. But it was not a court, few of the testimonies dragged on as long as a trial, and people coming before the commission were, for the most part, not facing sentence and had less need for lawyers.

Events in Zimbabwe, the Matabeleland massacres and the level of political violence from 2000 occurred on a much greater scale than that which had happened under apartheid, though both were tiny compared with the slaughter of 800 000 Rwandans. Zimbabwe already has a national debt of more than $6 billion,[10] and there will be other priorities to fund in the early days of a new government. A commission with any teeth is going to run for a long time and hear testimony from thousands of people. My own view is that the cost of the *Gukurahundi* trials should be carried by Britain – along with other Western countries – because of their silence at the time.

In 2002, BBC journalists Fergal Keane and Mark Dowd made a documentary for the *Panorama* programme in which they asked how much Whitehall had known about *Gukurahundi*. Sir Martin Ewans, who was high commissioner in Harare at the time, went on camera to say that his instructions from London were 'to steer clear of it' when speaking to Mugabe. 'I think that Matabeleland was a side issue,' he said. 'The real issues were much bigger. We were extremely interested that Zimbabwe should be a success story, and we were doing our best to help Mugabe and his people bring that about.'

His deputy, Roger Martin, actually witnessed some of the beatings, but agreed with his boss: 'The big picture involved keeping the show on the road for most of the country, recognising that this series of atrocities was happening in limited areas of Matabeleland, but not severing relations and watching the whole thing go down the tubes faster.'[11]

As for more recent events, it could be argued that the SADC countries – notably South Africa, which has so much leverage on Harare – should bear some of the cost because of their silence when those crimes where being committed.

Then there's the matter of reparation. This can be in the form of money, but there are many ways of helping the victims. In law, the terms that crop up most frequently are:

- **Restitution:** giving back what was lost by the criminal act. The accused may be ordered to rebuild a house they had burnt down or help those they forced into exile to re-establish themselves in Zimbabwe. The state may also be called on to hand back property and restore citizenship.
- **Compensation:** usually in the form of cash, but may include payment for lost education or unemployment, and recognition of mental and physical harm.

- **Rehabilitation:** medical and psychological care, and access to legal and social help.
- **Satisfaction:** the notion that justice must be seen to be done. It may also involve a search for the missing; reburial of the dead in accordance with local culture, especially where bodies were dumped in mass graves; acknowledgement of the facts; national apologies; healing ceremonies; memorials; and the passing of new laws to prevent the same crimes taking place again in the future.

One suggestion has been to confiscate ZANU-PF's considerable assets and use that money to pay for both a commission and its orders of compensation. In *The Battle for Zimbabwe*, I used documents from the International Monetary Fund and various NGOs to track the $5 billion that was allegedly spent on Zimbabwe's military adventures in the Democratic Republic of Congo, but since then more evidence has come to light.

In May 2004, former ZAPU fighters who had been loyal to the late Joshua Nkomo asked what had happened to the party's assets when Nkomo dissolved his organisation in 1987 and merged with ZANU-PF. They alleged that some of the ZAPU-owned firms had passed into the hands of Nkomo's senior aides, who went on to serve in the cabinet.

In the 2000 election, ZANU-PF had lost all but two of its seats in Matabeleland and was doing all it could to win back the province. Mugabe took the ZAPU claim seriously and ordered an inquiry. But there was mischief afoot. ZANU-PF was going through a factional war to sort out who might succeed Mugabe, and the inquiry offered the chance for rival candidates to taint each other with allegations of corruption.

First to go was the speaker of parliament, Emmerson Mnangagwa, widely tipped as next in line. He had allegedly overseen most of the party's forays into commerce, including a number of shady deals.

As stories leaked from the commission, the non-government weeklies revealed that ZANU-PF had built up a multi-billion-dollar empire through two investment vehicles: M&S Syndicate, which was set up before independence, and Zidco Holdings, whose board included Mnangagwa, defence minister Sydney Sekeremayi, and two Asian businessmen, Jayany Joshi and his brother, Manharlal.

The Joshi brothers fell out with their partners and fled to Britain, but stories of ZANU Inc. continued to surface. Shares had been transferred without authority, huge amounts of foreign exchange had been externalised, and some of Mugabe's closest allies were involved. Finance minister Christopher Kuruneri was exposed in the South African *Sunday Times* as owning a string of properties in Cape Town with a collective worth exceeding R8 million, along with a Mercedes Benz valued at R547 734 … all on a politician's salary.[12]

Kuruneri was arrested, but claimed he had earned the money in Spain and America before going into government. However, documents showed that in March 2002, while deputy minister of finance, he had withdrawn the equivalent of R5.2 million from Harare's Jewel Bank and sent it south without anyone noticing. A transaction of this size would, no doubt, have come to the attention of Jewel's chief executive, Gideon Gono, who was also alleged to be Mugabe's financial advisor and went on to become head of the Reserve Bank.

Gono was not investigated over the matter, the state drive against corruption quickly ran out of steam, the ZAPU allegations were not resolved, and several leading businessmen with links to the party were conveniently allowed to leave the country before warrants could be issued for their arrest. But what did emerge was that ZANU-PF owned or had shares in more than eighty companies, and that any real inquiry would lift the veil on years of greed and corruption that had created more than enough wealth to fund a truth and justice commission. Recovering the money could be more difficult.

In Kenya, the ruling KANU party of President Daniel arap Moi – in power since 1963 – lost the general election in 2002 to the Rainbow Coalition of former vice-president Mwai Kibaki. Within a year, the new government had traced just over a billion dollars that Moi and his cronies had stashed away overseas, but found that repatriating the money to Kenya was hell's own task.

Similar problems surfaced in Zambia, the DRC and Liberia, all countries that were looted by their former rulers. The new government in Nigeria was stalled at every turn when it tried to bring home an estimated $3 billion stolen by the late ruler Sani Abacha, who died in office in 1998, even when they tracked down some of the deposits in Citibank and Union Bancaire Privée in Switzerland.

'It's tough to get the money back,' according to André Pienaar, who oversees the African office of Kroll Inc., an international firm that has traced funds for many governments, including Kenya. 'Untangling a corrupt economy is a painful surgical process. It takes a long time and it's not always clear the patient will survive. These guys used some of the biggest, most respected banks to hide their money.'

In the case of Kenya, some of the cash was also used to buy foreign property, two London hotels, spacious homes in the English countryside and fleets of luxury cars.[13] Some who had made the purchases said they were 'simply following orders' from senior people and didn't know who ended up owning the assets.

But the problems in Nairobi don't end there. Two years after assuming power, donors are accusing the new Kibaki government of stealing as much as $500 million from the state through bribery, corruption and outright theft, and, they say, there is no sign that anyone is trying to stop the graft.

More than a million souls crowded into a park in Nairobi on 30 December 2002 to watch an event once thought impossible: Daniel arap Moi handing over power to the democratically elected government of people's hero Mwai Kibaki.

'The happy new era', as it was known, started well, and the country was hailed as an example of what could be done in the wake of theft and tyranny.

- A policy of free primary education sent 1.2 million children back to school.
- The judiciary was purged and twenty-three members of the bench were suspended when a report accused them of adjusting their verdicts in exchange for bribes and sexual favours.
- Anti-corruption laws forced public servants to declare their assets.
- Donor countries that had shunned Moi's government pledged billions in aid.

In the last year of Moi's rule, Transparency International (TI) had ranked Kenya the sixth most corrupt country on earth. In response, one of Kibaki's first moves was to place the head of TI Kenya, thirty-seven-year-old John Githongo, in charge of a new anti-graft squad that would answer directly to the president.

Shortly after the change, a worldwide Gallup poll rated Kenyans the most optimistic people on earth, but, all too soon, the revolution lost its way.[14]

John Githongo started feeling the heat when, instead of just unravelling deals done while Moi was in charge, he also focused on the new cabinet; but, try as he might, Githongo could not get Kibaki to move against his own.

In July 2004, the British high commissioner to Nairobi, Sir Edward Clay, accused Kibaki ministers and officials of embezzling £125 million in state funds, and said he had passed on names to the president. Clay and Githongo were good friends and there was little doubt where the diplomat had obtained his information.

'We may wake up one day at the end of this giant looting spree,' Clay warned, 'to find Kenya's potential is all behind us and that it is a land of lost opportunity.'[15]

The government was outraged and chastised the high commissioner for his remarks, but Britain was joined by other key investors, including the United States and Japan, who complained that things were slipping back to the bad old ways.

Unfazed, Kibaki began undermining Githongo's work, and when Margaret Gachara, director of the National AIDS Control Council, was jailed for defrauding the government of $340 000, he pardoned her, along with 7 000 other offenders who had stolen funds from various government offices.

In February 2005, Githongo fled to London from where he resigned his post, claiming that he could not stay in Kenya because those he had exposed were still at large and threatening to kill him.[16]

The poverty and unemployment that marked the Moi era hadn't improved either. Two years on, the government claimed that half a million new jobs had been created, but, according to local economists, the job market had shrunk. And, to top it all, the Russian mafia had moved in and Nairobi was fast becoming a hub of international crime.[17]

Mwai Kibaki knew the KANU way of doing things, having spent ten years (1978–1988) as vice-president under Daniel arap Moi. Should Zimbabwe be worried that most of the MDC leadership, including Morgan Tsvangirai, was once loyal members of ZANU-PF?

Kenya's story is not unique. When Zambia's Kenneth Kaunda and Malawi's 'life president' Hastings Banda conceded to demands for multiparty government and were trounced at the polls, the leaders who replaced them interfered with the press, did little to relieve unemployment and were accused of embezzlement.

But perhaps the worst case was that of Eritrea's President Isayas Afewerki. Professor Makau Mutua teaches law at the State University of New York and also chairs the Kenya Human Rights Commission, and he has written widely on Eritrea and how far the country has slid down the scale of tyranny.

> What is shocking is that Mr Afewerki, dubbed in the 1990s by the Clinton administration as one of a new breed of African leaders, has turned out to be more Mobutu Sese Seko of Zaire and nothing like Nelson Mandela of South Africa.
>
> Eritrea was much admired both in Africa and the West after it gained freedom from an oppressive and backward Ethiopian state. Led by the then popular Mr Afewerki, Eritreans and their supporters abroad viewed the new state as a *tabula rasa* [a blank slate] on which a utopian democracy would be established, a shining example to other African states, but Mr Afewerki has dashed those hopes.
>
> In 1997, after Eritreans ratified the country's first democratic constitution, Mr Afewerki refused to promulgate it. He has rejected free elections, and now rules by fiat. Since 2001, he has instituted a sweeping crackdown on democratic reformers and outspoken government critics. He has detained without trial senior government officials. Afewerki has closed down all independent media and employed the Judiciary as an instrument of repression.[18]

In Africa, liberating a country from the old guard is tough enough, but keeping the new rulers honest can be a bitch.

8

Never Again?

To be free is not merely to cast off one's chains, but to live in a way that respects and enhances the freedom of others.

– Nelson Mandela

THE REDRESS TRUST IN LONDON, REFERRED TO IN THE previous chapter, has drawn up a list for what it calls 'A Guarantee of Non-Repetition' – safeguards that would make it harder for new governments to veer off track. These include:

- effective civilian control of the military;
- an independent judiciary;
- protecting the work of human rights defenders;
- ethical codes of conduct for government workers, especially the police and prisons service;
- promotion of a strong civil society.[1]

But what can be done if a new government – like ZANU-PF in 1980 – starts out with talk of progress and reconciliation and only later turns into a monster? Judging by Africa's record, not much!

One of the problems in maintaining democracy in the Third World is that heads of state are so tolerant of their erring colleagues in other countries. Mugabe has survived, in part, because neighbouring states, notably South Africa, have been reticent to act against him or even to criticise his record on human rights.

And this is not limited to the ANC. The old National Party

took no interest in *Gukurahundi*, and few of the white liberals who now complain about Thabo Mbeki's policy of 'quiet diplomacy' raised their voices in the 1980s, when Mugabe nationalised the press and murdered the Matabele.

But it was the ANC that had fought so hard to bring democracy to South Africa, and this makes it all the more strange that ministers with impeccable credentials in the struggle now remain silent. The rights of Africans to life, liberty and the pursuit of happiness extend, it would seem, only as far north as the Limpopo.

One wonders: if Mandela had been an Eritrean jailed by Afewerki, or if Steve Biko, who was murdered by South African police in 1977, had instead been born in Zimbabwe and was tortured to death by the CIO, would the ANC have taken up their cause?

South Africa, and especially Mbeki, has done exceptional work trying to secure peace for Liberia, Côte d'Ivoire, the Democratic Republic of Congo, Sudan and Burundi, but the effort came long after citizens in those countries had first cried out for help against repressive governments.

By contrast, in the 1999 elections in Austria, when far-right politician Joerg Haider took 20.6 per cent of the vote and his racist Freedom Party joined the ruling coalition, the European Union slapped diplomatic sanctions on Vienna and suspended the government from many of the EU's decision-making bodies.

The elections had been free and fair and Austrians had made their democratic choice, but defenders of the ban claimed that the EU was a body of 'shared values' and that racism and xenophobia were not on the list, and conflicted with the Universal Declaration of Human Rights and a host of other treaties that the European parliament had ratified.

But the African Union has made no such moves against patently murderous governments and, tragically, their silence is not unique. The Organisation of American States has often been criticised for going soft when members like Venezuela or Peru, let alone Cuba, crack down on protesters or try to muzzle the press. Equally, the countries of South Asia are frequently at loggerheads with the EU over their apparent acceptance of the military junta in Burma.

Brussels had imposed sanctions on the Burmese leadership not dissimilar to those applied to Zimbabwe: an arms embargo, as well as a visa ban and asset freeze. But, in November 2004, when the EU wanted Burma banned from regular trade talks known as the Asia–Europe Meeting, Asian countries took an all-or-nothing stand, insisting that the Rangoon government be part of the forum.

There are some who argue that international values on democracy and human rights, drawn up largely in the West, are not as applicable in countries like Zimbabwe or Eritrea, but Morgan Tsvangirai disagrees.

'Nothing, absolutely nothing, should be classified as an *African standard*, different from what happens elsewhere,' he told an audience in Johannesburg in January 2005, adding that his party wanted Africa to be 'a continent that respects universal principles on all facets of human endeavour'.[2]

Moeletsi Mbeki, vice chairman of the South African Institute of International Affairs, agrees. 'Africans are, of course, no different from other human beings in that they also want security and comfort. What is happening, however, is that the great majority of Africans are today experiencing the opposite; less security and comfort, and in many instances they face hunger, homelessness, threats of violence and actual violence, and starvation on a daily basis.'[3]

But if Kenya and Eritrea, Zambia and Malawi show what can go wrong in the wake of liberation, are there countries that Zimbabwe might emulate in order to get it right?

At more than twice the size of France, the former French colony of Mali is the second largest country in West Africa. In 1991, after twenty-three years of dictatorial rule by Moussa Traore, General Amadou Toumani Touré assumed power in a bloodless coup and, bucking the trend of military rulers, steered the country to democratic elections in which he refused to stand.

Alpha Oumar Konare was elected president, served his maximum of two five-year terms and stepped down in 2002, when General Touré took over with 64 per cent of the vote.

In 1991, Mali was one of the poorest and most oppressive countries on earth, but within a decade it had become an example for the rest of Africa. According to the US State Department's *Report on Human Rights Practices* for 2003, there were no incidents of arbitrary or unlawful deprivation of life, politically motivated disappearances, torture or political prisoners.

Corruption, which had permeated every aspect of national life, was also on the wane. 'No other African country has fought corruption like Mali,' says Pascal Kambale, counsel for the International Justice Programme at Human Rights Watch in Washington. 'The Ministry of Justice has undertaken an ambitious legal reform programme to bring about transparency. Mali does not only need legal expertise; the international community should lend greater financial assistance to guarantee this programme's success.'[4]

On the other side of the continent lies Somalia, a country where competing warlords like Mohamed Farah Aideed filled the vacuum left by government. But in the north, in what used to be British Somaliland until it merged with the Italian-occupied south at independence in 1960, a miracle is under way.

When Somalia collapsed in 1991 on the overthrow of dictator Siad Barre, the northern sector reinstated the colonial boundary and declared itself independent. Increasingly, Africa and the world treat the country as a sovereign state, though by 2005, no one had granted formal recognition.

In the new Republic of Somaliland, with its capital in the northern city of Hargiesa, elections are transparent and hotly contested; the media is largely independent; citizens have unfettered access to the Internet; and, in November 2004, even Amnesty International had praise for the country, commenting in one report that 'Somaliland has been the only part of the former Somali Republic to have achieved a broad measure of peace and stability under a civilian multiparty system.'[5]

Mali, Somaliland and, of course, South Africa, show that sustaining democracy is possible if the structures are in place and people of good faith lead the way.

In Zimbabwe, a new constitution should be put to a referendum, with the safeguard that the document could only be altered through another public vote.

The constitution should include clauses that will:

- maintain media freedom;
- ban torture;
- create space for the opposition;
- guarantee a high level of personal liberty; and
- reconcile the nation.

Consideration should also be given to women's issues, care for the aged, minority rights, and, as has happened in South Africa, a host of clauses that bar discrimination on grounds of gender, race, age, handicap or sexual orientation. South Africa is the only country in the world where gay rights are protected by the Constitution.

In the parliament of Zimbabwe, MPs may vote against their own party, and sometimes do, but the constitution bans a member from defecting permanently by crossing the floor, a provision that should stay in order to prevent the ruling party from using the lure of a position in government to poach MPs from the other side.

But the rule on by-elections could be changed. At present, if a sitting MP dies or retires, a fresh election is held in that constituency, allowing the ruling party to pump state funds into the district and so distort the outcome. A better practice, widely used around the world, allows the former MP's party to select a replacement to hold the seat until the next election. And the current clause allowing the president to appoint thirty 'non-constituency' MPs of his own choice will also have to go.

The death penalty is certain to come up for discussion, having been banned across much of the continent, including ten states in West Africa, and in Angola, Mauritius, Mozambique, Namibia and South Africa. While it is still on the books in Kenya, Malawi and Zambia, the presidents of those countries have said they will not enforce it.[6]

The Rhodesian government was notorious for executing its opponents, and from 1980 to 2005, more than seventy people were hanged in Zimbabwe, mostly for heinous crimes. For example, in three cases since 2000, the death penalty was carried out on:

- Edmore Masendeke, for his part in the 1995 murder of an elderly widow, Eileen Carlisle, in the southern town of Masvingo, although his accomplice escaped with a fifteen-year jail sentence after turning state witness.
- Anthony Muuzhe, for the murder of two children, burnt to death when he set fire to their hut and wired the door shut, hoping to kill their mother.
- Noel Rukanda, for raping and strangling a fourteen-year-old girl.

Opponents of capital punishment argue that it cannot be undone if the guilty verdict is found to have been wrong, which, it seems, happens all too often. In the United States, for example, of 500 men and women executed between 1977 and 1997, seventy-five – or around one in six – were later proved innocent.[7]

And, according to research, the death penalty holds little deterrent value. Criminals are concerned about the risk of being caught, and if this is low – in Johannesburg, one in every ten serious crimes leads to an arrest – the threat of being executed might not worry a would-be villain.

Before World War II, Rhodesia had abolished trial by jury, replacing it with a system in which cases were heard by a judge and two assessors. Under the old rules, the defence and prosecution jointly selected twelve jurors, making it harder for government to sway the verdict. The legal profession might do well to consider reinstating the jury system.

Whatever a future government decides on the death penalty and juries, the bigger challenge will be to clean up the prison system.

In 2004, a US State Department report on Zimbabwe was scathing about the level of abuse suffered by those in jail, describing conditions behind bars as 'harsh and life threatening'.

The forty-seven prisons, it said, were designed for 16 000 inmates but held 25 000 in overcrowded conditions, with shortages of food and clothing, and without proper sanitation. AIDS was a major cause of death, and the infection rate in jail was close to 60 per cent.

Pre-trial delays were a problem, and a shortage of magistrates and court interpreters meant that detainees spent up to four years in custody before going to court. By 2005, there was a backlog of 60 000 cases.[8]

These conditions fell well outside international standards of care for prisoners, and allowed the ruling party to terrorise its opponents with the spectre of arrest and detention.

In October 2004, a parliamentary committee voted along

party lines to jail MDC member of parliament Roy Bennett after he had pushed justice minister Patrick Chinamasa during a heated debate in the house of assembly.

The rule that allows parliament to act as a court against its own members is unusual and out of step with international law, but the committee sentenced Bennett to twelve months with hard labour.

The MP was initially held in Harare, but was later moved to a remote prison in Mutoko, 145 kilometres east of the capital, and allowed only a fortnightly visit from his wife Heather. In cramped conditions, Bennett was frequently ill and underfed, and complained of lice-infected blankets and poor sanitation. The only relief was that his fluency in Shona and celebrity status, after attacking the unpopular Chinamasa, made him a hero among fellow inmates, who did their best to care for him.[9]

While a free Zimbabwe is likely to abolish the right of MPs to jail their own, it is the conditions in prison that need to be addressed, so that if a person at odds with the state is jailed for any reason, the punishment does not become unusually cruel or degrading.

Changing laws is one thing, but it is also important that, years from now, people still remember what had happened and remain vigilant in case a future government gets heavy-handed.

In the Preface, I spoke of my visit to Rwanda in 2004, ten years after the genocide. As guest lecturer for the master's degree programme at the University of Pretoria's faculty of human rights law, I found no shortage of students and lecturers with strong views on justice and the defence of freedom. And there we were, together at the Gorilla Hotel in the capital, Kigali, eager to see how this tiny nation had survived a holocaust and rebuilt itself as a successful African state.

Over the next few days we visited countless sites where the killings had taken place, and, for all the theory, lectures, workshops, videos and news clips of the genocide, none of us was ready for what we saw.

To make sure no one forgets what happened and to counter the denials of those who claim it was all an exaggeration, the new government of Paul Kagame has left tens of thousands of skeletons where they fell, ghoulish monuments to the dead.

In one school, where children had sheltered in classrooms, the tiny bones of infants still at kindergarten were grouped in categories and stacked on shelves. Skulls the size of grapefruit, ribs no bigger than the fingers that held the machetes whose blades were brought down with such force on the living flesh that some of the skulls were cleaved in half, arms and legs cut through, the pieces now placed together in room after room piled high with all that remains of the children who had once sat here in class.

In a church at Ntarama, about a two-hour drive from Kigali, the bones of adults were mixed with those of children who had huddled behind their parents as the Interhamwe militia broke down the door. Now the bones lay a foot deep on the floor and, as I walked down the aisle, they crunched under my feet.

But it was a field behind one of the chapels that chilled me the most. Here, large black bags, the kind I use at home for garbage, were filled with the skulls and bones of those who had hidden in the grounds and been hunted down. Gross as they were, the displays in schoolrooms and between the pews had a sense of decorum, but here, in hundreds of refuse bags, in an empty field, there was no dignity for those who had perished. People like me; people like you.

Even so, the bags told a story. At other memorials, like the one at Butare University in the south, where Tutsi students and their teachers were butchered, the bodies have been buried and a small museum stands over the grave. How many bodies? Only God knows.

On the road to Butare there is another mass grave, containing some 20 000 corpses, or so the sign says. But, like the Nazi holocaust, there will be deniers, if not now, then in the future, rewriting history with the claim that the tales of atrocity have been fabricated by those bent on vilifying the old regime. Even in Russia, there are some who think fondly of Stalin.

But in Rwanda, denying the truth will be a hard task while the bones remain unburied and on view in the churches and schools, and this made me wonder what kind of memorials Zimbabwe should erect to the past in an effort to secure a better future.

When I returned from Kigali, I showed my photographs to a number of Matabele people now living in Johannesburg, all of whom had lost friends and family during *Gukurahundi*. Some felt that it was foreign to black culture for bones to be left in public instead of being given a proper burial. Others, like Jabulani Mkwanazi, who lost family members in the genocide, believed that at least some of the mass graves should be opened and the remains put on public display.

'There are special circumstances for things like this,' said Jabu, who is now chairman of the MDC in Johannesburg. 'We are talking about the cold-blooded murder of tens of thousands of people in Matabeleland, and future generations must know that it happened and be able to see the horror of what took place.

'Memorials are one thing and survivors can be there to tell you what happened, but the evidence lies under the ground, and I would have no problem with my family's bones being used in a display before being given a decent reburial, if this is what it takes to make sure Zimbabwe never goes down that road again.'

In Johannesburg, the Apartheid Museum houses a balanced and well-documented record of South African history from 1947 to 1994. With photos, newsreels, posters, clippings and even a replica of a solitary confinement cell, it brings home the lunacy and horror of a policy doomed to failure.

In Zimbabwe, perhaps the CIO headquarters, a red-brick office block near parliament, could be turned into a museum. Here torture devices, propaganda reels and photographs of burnt-out homes that had once belonged to those who stood against the regime could be displayed, along with personal testimonies on tape and in print, so that people of all ages can see what happened.

And at least one of the youth brigade camps, where so many were tortured and brainwashed, should also be maintained as a monument to madness: *Lest we forget!*

In Rwanda, I was disturbed at how the Hutu people, who were dominated by the Tutsis for almost 500 years, had been largely written out of the country's history, except as perpetrators of genocide. Their story should also be on show if the country is to learn the full cause of what went wrong and if history is not to become what Winston Churchill famously described as 'propaganda written by the winners'.

Perhaps in Zimbabwe, professional historians and museum experts from other countries could add an impartial voice by being asked to join the teams that set up the memorial displays.

The MDC, both at home and in exile, has committed human rights abuses, though certainly not on the scale of the crimes laid at the door of ZANU-PF. Even so, I have heard testimony of torture carried out by the opposition, and have no doubt that three high-profile killings of local ZANU-PF leaders – Ali Khan Mangengwa in Harare, and Limukani Lupahla and Cain Nkala in Matabeleland – were the work of MDC members.[10] I have found no evidence to suggest that the killings were sanctioned on high, but even so, if our story is meant as a warning for the future, we have to start with the truth.

Whoever eventually brings freedom to Zimbabwe, whether it be the MDC, a coalition government, a new party not yet established or even a reformed ZANU-PF, when the celebrations die down and the hard business of government begins, there should be no honeymoon period during which the new government is treated leniently.

From day one, the nation, the media, NGOs, human rights groups, neighbouring states and the world must hold the new rulers to account, making sure that, in Zimbabwe, Africa finds a model that others will be proud to follow.

When Rhodesia came to an end and the transition to democracy offered so much promise, Zimbabwean songwriter Clem Tholet penned a ballad called 'Peace Dream',[11] in which he spoke of a better future, where the past was forgiven and people of all colours and tribes worked together to build their place in the sun.

Clem died in 2004 at the age of just fifty-six, but his words form a fitting close to this book and will, I hope, one day become a prayer for Africa, and especially for Zimbabwe.

> May the mountains standing by you ever guard you,
> And the rivers wash your spirit bright and clean;
> May the animals and birds sing of the peace that is to come
> And not the glory of a land that might have been.
> May the lives that you have taken be for a reason,
> And the pain that you have suffered make you strong.
> May the seeds that you have sown bring out the fullness of
>   the future
> May God give you the strength to right your wrongs.
> It's just a dream, I know – but dreams set you free
> Dreaming can ease your mind … and bring you peace.
> May the sweetness of your soil yet bring you riches,
> And your pastures ever fill your belly's needs.
> May the nations that you harbour find a way to live as one;
> Keep your standards high, do not give in to greed.
> May God be with you and keep you strong;
> May your tomorrows be rich and long.

Clem Tholet: 1950–2004

Epilogue

Does Zimbabwe Hold any Lessons for South Africa?

IN RESEARCHING THIS BOOK AND IN THE MANY LECTURES I delivered while promoting the previous title, people invariably asked me the same two questions: When will better days come to Zimbabwe, and will the collapse of that country be repeated in South Africa?

To the first I have no answer, except to say that, when change comes, it will probably take us by surprise, which is all the more reason to be prepared.

On South Africa, my comments disappoint those who want to hear that all will be well. The potential for disaster looms large in the Rainbow Nation and most, I fear, are searching in the wrong place for answers.

So where *do* you begin? I'd start at Jo'burg's Park Station and the long-haul buses pulling in from all over the country, each one packed with young men and women from the rural areas in search of a better life.

The problem is so bad that, if the rate of migration to cities like Johannesburg and Durban is not stemmed, urban life – including jobs, water, housing and general well-being – will not keep pace with the surge in population. In this, South Africa is not unique, as the problem is just as severe in Thailand, the Philippines,

Kenya and Brazil, and in each case the typical migrant is aged between eighteen and thirty, educated … and unemployed.

Studies by the United Nations and others have shown that, when you educate people in the countryside, they invariably move to town. One report suggested that, after three years of primary school, a person was twice as likely to seek work in the city than someone with no education. After three years at high school, the ratio doubled again to four times!

Mugabe's problems in the late 1990s started in the black slums around Harare, Mutare, Bulawayo and other cities, where educated blacks in their late teens and early twenties lived in poverty and hunger, angry at a government that didn't seem to care. It was from here that the first riots erupted. When the MDC started out, it was an urban party that spoke to the needs of the poor and unemployed. Land never featured in the debate until Mugabe started seizing farms in the hope that he could fend off the pack by handing out plots they hadn't asked for in the first place.

As I write these words in Johannesburg, there are no riots in South Africa and the ruling African National Congress is so popular that, in the 2004 election, the party scored a two-thirds majority in parliament. But South Africa has one of the most rapidly urbanising societies on earth, and every year more school-leavers spill into a shrinking job market, and thousands who have gained their education in rural areas move to town, literate, numerate and high on expectation.

And nothing will lure them back to the land.

In 2005, a Johannesburg firm, Research Surveys, agreed to help me write this Epilogue by polling South Africans for their views on various issues. Neil Higgs, a director of the company, worked out some questions, and in March he showed me the answers.

A total of 2 000 people were surveyed in seven metropolitan areas, and the first two questions were designed to test how strongly black South Africans living in town were tied to urban life. I have summarised the results below, but you can see them in greater detail on Research Survey's website, www.researchsurveys.co.za/.

Question One

The polling team asked blacks to choose between working in town or owning a plot in the country.

Which would you prefer: a paid job in the city, or your own piece of land in a rural area?

- Paid job in town 82%
- Land 18%

The size of the plots on offer was then specified in an effort to test how strongly respondents would hold to their first answer, but, in this case, size didn't matter.

- 10 hectares in a rural area 5%
- 20 hectares 4%
- 50 hectares 3%
- 100 hectares 6%

The 100-hectare option had a slightly higher preference among men than women (8 per cent vs. 5 per cent), but the numbers suggested that, once in town, few would consider leaving.

But what if you didn't need a job? Where would you then choose to live?

Question Two

If you won more than R5 m (±$800 000) in the lottery and no longer had to work, would you prefer to make your home in the city or in the countryside?

- Blacks : City 68%, Country 32%
- Whites: City 54%, Country 46%

It was interesting to see how many whites were attracted to rural life as opposed to black respondents. Among other groups, 67 per cent of coloureds and 79 per cent of Indians opted for town.

Question three

Next, we tested views on the media, which Mugabe nationalised in 1982. How did South Africans feel when the press tackled those in power?

Should the media be critical if they feel that the government is doing something wrong?

Among the respondents, 85 percent said '**yes**', with only a slight variation among race groups:

- Whites 91%
- Indians 90%
- Coloureds 86%
- Blacks 83%

Other issues

In other questions, 80 percent of all races and 74 percent of blacks felt that, where land was obtained for redistribution, it should be utilised solely for that purpose and that none should be handed over to ministers or government officials for their own use.

In a separate poll on Zimbabwe, Research Surveys found that only 14 percent of South Africans felt that Mugabe's approach to land redistribution should be applied to their country, with no significant difference of opinion between blacks and whites.

Finally, in the survey done for this book, 72 percent of blacks were tolerant of black people from elsewhere on the continent making their home in South Africa, whereas only 52 percent of whites liked the idea.

In time, Research Surveys will expand this line of questioning by sampling people in rural areas on their views about land and jobs, but in the cities, at least, the results so far suggest that urban growth will continue and that few will be drawn back to the land, no matter what.

My own view is that the government should embark on a major campaign of decentralisation, encouraging business to set up in smaller towns around the country. Tax breaks, free industrial land and progressive town councils are needed to make it work, but the results can be significant and, if young people can find jobs in their own communities, it will curb the explosion taking place in Gauteng and make it easier for rural families to stay together.

In Chapter 4, I touched on the ambivalence some black Zimbabweans feel towards the white farmers, and, from the little work I have done in rural South Africa, I fear for the future.

There seems to be a brutish intolerance among some white farming communities, who pump out the worst kind of PR for their cause. It is understandable that families who have worked the land for generations should resist government efforts to buy up their farms for redistribution, and the process of resettlement in South Africa has been flawed, with too many of the new black farmers unable to cope, and once-productive estates going to ruin.

But white farmers need to sell the message that keeping them on the land is good for the country and, at present, I see little sign of them doing this.

As time goes by, if the ANC maintains its excellent record on rural education, land will become even less of an issue for most black South Africans. But, ironically, the new, more canny and vocal generation armed with high school certificates and dreams of a better life may challenge the very party that sent them to class.

If the ANC lays good plans now for an urban future, the wave of discontent that rose up against Mugabe might still be avoided. Like Mauritius, which enjoys zero unemployment, South Africa could become an industrial giant to challenge the Asian Tigers.

Since 1994, the ANC has delivered the most democratic society in the history of Africa, but, if the government fails to create urban jobs for the new generation, its days are numbered.

Democracy is not measured by a political party's desire for power, but by the acceptance that, every now and then, the electorate has the right to send the incumbents into opposition. If that day comes for the ANC, I have no doubt that, as in Zimbabwe, the issues will be urban poverty and unemployment. Whether South Africa slips into tragedy will depend on those who rule at the time, and how willing they are to accept the people's verdict.

Notes

CHAPTER 1

1 (a) *Measuring Poverty*: World Bank, 1999, http://www.worldbank.org/poverty/mission/up2.htm0.
(b) The $ symbol is used throughout to denote American currency. References to the Zimbabwean dollar appear as Z$, followed by the figure.

2 *Cost of War*: http://costofwar.com

3 *Boston Globe*, 25 March 2002.

4 *A Problem from Hell, America in the Age of Genocide*: Samantha Power. London: Flamingo Books in association with HarperCollins, 2003.

5 Latin Focus Economic Data 2004: http://www.latin-focus.com

6 All currency is Zimbabwean, except the tourism figures, which represent US dollars.

7 *African Tears* newsletter: Cathy Buckle, 4 September 2004.

8 'Fighting the AIDS Epidemic by Issuing Condoms in the Prisons': Brent Staple, *New York Times*, 7 September 2004.

9 *Washington Times*, 9 March 2004.

10 'Secrets of the Camps': *BBC Panorama*, February 2004.

11 *We Wish to Inform You that Tomorrow We Will be Killed With Our Families – Memories from Rwanda*: Philip Gourevitch. New York: Farrar, Strauss and Giroux, 1998.

12 'Biafra Thirty Years On': Barnaby Phillips, *BBC*, 13 January 2000.

CHAPTER 2

1 Raath is one of three foreign correspondents who quit Zimbabwe in February 2005 after being secretly warned that they were about to be arrested on trumped-up charges of spying and forex contraventions. Their office in Harare was raided and they were harassed at their homes in the days prior to their hasty departure. All three were Zimbabwean citizens.

2 'Zimbabwe's Once-proud Schools Face Ruin': Jan Raath, *The Times* (London), 1 June 2004.

3 'State Buys Prados for Defence Chiefs': *The Standard* (Harare), 22 August, 2004.

4 *Harassment and Torture of Students and Teachers*: Amnesty International, November 2002.
5 *Our Path to Social Justice*: RESTART, Movement for Democratic Change (Harare), 2004.
6 'Ministers and Unruly Pupils Causing Collapse of Schools': John Clare (education editor), *Daily Telegraph* (London), 27 May 2004.
7 International Organisation for Migration, 2002.
8 *United Nations Development Report*, 2004, quoted in *The Zimbabwe Independent*, 8 October 2004.
9 *Ibid.*
10 Faculty of Medicine, University of Newfoundland (Canada), 2004.

CHAPTER 3

1 Most townships do have electricity, but the residents can't pay the bills, so power is invariably disconnected.
2 *A Field Guide to the Snakes of Southern Africa*: Dr VFM FitzSimons. London: Collins, 1970.
3 *Zimbabwe: Police Place Human Rights Under Siege*: Amnesty International (London), 5 May 2004.
4 *Victims of Torture*: Eric Beauchemin broadcast, 16 May 2002.
5 *Country Report for Zimbabwe – January to December 2001*: Amnesty International (New York), 2002.
6 *Preliminary Report*: Commonwealth Observer Group: Presidential Election in Zimbabwe, 14 March 2002.
7 *Africa Report*: Amnesty International Medical Team, 6 June 2003.
8 'Daily News Editor Charged Under POSA': Blessing Zulu, *The Independent* (Harare), 27 June 2003.
9 *Policing to Protect Human Rights: A Survey of Police Practice in Countries of the SADC 1997–2002*: Amnesty International (London), 2002.
10 *Sowetan*, 29 November 2004.
11 United Nations Resolution 56/143, 19 December 2001, para 2.
12 *Policing to Protect Human Rights*: Amnesty International.
13 Human Rights Watch, August 2004.
14 'High Court Judge Quizzed by Secret Service Agents': *ZimOnline*, 27 August 2004.
15 'Rule of the Lawless': Jan Raath, *The Spectator* (UK), 21 August 2004.
16 'Inefficiency Skews the Scales of Justice': *The Citizen*, 3 November 2004.

CHAPTER 4

1 *Blood and Soil. Land, Politics and Conflict Prevention in Zimbabwe and South Africa*: International Crisis Group (Brussels), 2004.
2 Made up of two or more overlapping circles and often used in mathematics to show relationships between sets, similarities and differences.
3 *Harvest of Thorns*: Shimmer Chinodya. Harare: Baobab Books, 1989; *The Rain Goddess*: Peter Stiff. Salisbury: Jacaranda Press, 1973 and Johannesburg: Galago, 2004; *Selous Scouts Top Secret War*: Lt Col Ron Reid-Daly. Johannesburg: Galago, 1982 and Johannesburg: Covos-Day Books, 1999, reprinted 2000; *None But Ourselves*: Julie Frederikse. Harare: Zimbabwe Publishing House, 1982.
4 'Farmland Lies Fallow: *IRIN* (United Nations), 31 May 2004.
5 *The Battle for Zimbabwe*: Geoff Hill. Cape Town: Zebra Press, 2003.
6 Sent to the author by Justice for Agriculture, March 2005.
7 *Blood and Soil: Land, Politics and Conflict Prevention in Zimbabwe and South Africa*: International Crisis Group.
8 *The Economist*, 6 November 2003.
9 Agri-SA media statement, 31 January 2003.
10 *The Citizen*, 11 December 2004.
11 *Afrol News*, 23 October 2004.
12 *Blood and Soil*: International Crisis Group.
13 *WFP Zimbabwe Country Info*: www.wfp.org/country_brief/index.asp?region=3
14 *ZimOnline*, 25 December 2004.
15 'Zimbabwe Loses Out on High-profit Farm': *Business Day*, 17 May 2004.
16 *The Herald* (Harare), 5 November 2004.
17 'Heavy Debt and Drought Drive India's Farmers to Desperation': Amy Waldman, *New York Times*, 18 June 2004.

CHAPTER 5

1 *Freedom of the Press 2004 – A Global Survey of Media Independence*: New York: Freedom House, 28 April 2004.
2 *Press Freedom Index*: Reporters Sans Frontiéres (Paris), 2004.
3 'Plan to Tame Journalists Just Stirs Them Up in Brazil': Larry Rohter, *New York Times*, 6 September 2004.
4 'Portrait of Bush Using Apes Creates a Stir': *Reuters*, 15 December 2004.
5 'Mugabe Introduces New Curbs on Internet': Andrew Meldrum, *The Guardian* (UK), 3 June 2004.
6 'Zimbabwe Outlaws Satirical Play': *BBC News*, 11 May 2004.
7 Taken from a speech delivered by Australian foreign minister Alexander Downer MP at the

Commonwealth Press Union biennial conference in Sydney, Australia on 23 February 2005.

CHAPTER 6

1 Mark Twain, whose real name was Samuel Langhorne Clemens, travelled widely, even visiting South Africa, and often made jokes about the French.
2 'The development potential of Zimbabweans in the diaspora'. A survey of Zimbabweans living in the UK and South Africa. Alice Bloch, the International Organisation for Migration, March 2005.
3 'You Are Not Alone: Big Brother is Watching You More Closely Than Ever': Caroline Hooper-Box, *Sunday Independent* (SA), 23 January 2005.
4 'UK Probes Immigration Scam by Zim Asylum Seekers': *The Standard* (Harare), 27 June 2004.
5 'Trying to Stem Tide of African Migrants is Futile, says Blair': Paul Eastham, *Daily Mail*, 31 December 2004.
6 *Encyclopaedia Britannica*, 2005.
7 'Visa Scams Proliferate as Zimbabweans Seek to Flee': Angela Makamure, *eAfrica News* (South Africa), 2 June 2004.
8 'There Are Too Many Immigrants, say 75 per cent of Britons': Philip Johnston, *Daily Telegraph* (London), 10 December 2004.
9 'Immigration: New Scandal': Kirsty Walker, *Daily Express*, 17 June 2004.
10 'Tories Make Asylum Cost a Poll Issue': George Jones and Robert Shrimsley, *Daily Telegraph* (London), 7 June 2000.
11 'Asylum Case Backlog Costs Taxpayer £500m': Philip Johnston, *Daily Telegraph* (London), 8 February 2005.
12 'NHS is Hit by £200m HIV Bill': James Slack, *Daily Mail*, 24 June 2005.
13 'Britain a Foreign Land': David Cracknell, *Daily Telegraph* (London), 4 March 2001.
14 Advertisement for Fellowes shredding machines, *The Times*, 23 September 2004.
15 'Tories Make Asylum Cost a Poll Issue': *Daily Telegraph.*
16 'Trying to Stem Tide of African Migrants': *Daily Mail.*
17 'Howard Puts Immigration at Heart of Election Battle': Patrick Hennessy, *Sunday Telegraph*, 23 January 2005.
18 *Ibid.*
19 'Dawn Raids Smash £1m Visa Scam': Greg Swift, *Daily Express*, 17 June 2004.
20 'Internet Shoppers Click up a £2.6 bn Bill over Christmas': *Daily Mail*, 30 December 2004.
21 'Chip and Pin Society': *Daily Mail*, 30 December 2004.
22 'Half of all Recruits to Army Read at Level of 11-year-olds':

Sean Rayment, *Daily Telegraph*, 28 March 2004.

22 'The development potential of Zimbabweans in the diaspora': Alice Bloch.

24 'Dual Citizenship Analysed': Frederick W Jjuuko, *Uganda Human Rights Commission Magazine* (Kampala), May 2003.

25 'NHS too Dependent on Agency Nurses': Nic Fleming, *Daily Telegraph*, 2 November 2004.

CHAPTER 7

1 *Guinness Book of World Records*, London, 2003.

2 'General Pinochet's Day In Court': *New York Times*, 7 September 2004.

3 'We'll Break Some Bones in Pursuit of War Criminals': Harry de Quetteville, *Daily Telegraph*, 22 January 2005.

4 'Gaçaca Courts Roll Out Across Rwanda': *Hirondelle News Agency* (Arusha), 4 February 2005.

5 *Sierra Leone: War Crimes Court Impeded by Lack of Funds*: Human Rights Watch (New York), 8 September 2004.

6 *Zimbabwe: From Impunity to Accountability*: The Redress Trust (London), March 2004: www.redress.org

7 Rudolf Hoess built Auschwitz and later ran the inspectorate which oversaw all the concentration camps. Not to be confused with Hitler's deputy, Rudolf Hess, who fled to Britain in 1941. Hoess's candid autobiography, *Commandant of Auschwitz*, written during his trial, was reprinted in 2005 by the Orion Publishing Group, London.

8 'Abuse Defense : Following Orders': Pete Williams, *NBC News* (New York), 6 May 2004.

9 'Germans Mark 60th Anniversary of Dresden Fire Bombing': *Agence France Presse*, 13 February 2005.

10 *The Standard* (Harare), 22 February 2004.

11 *BBC Panorama*, 10 March 2002.

12 'Zimbabwe Forex Scam Raises More Questions': *Sunday Times* (SA), 16 May 2004.

13 'Kenya Joins Nations Pursuing Funds Stolen by Ex-leaders': Marc Lacey, *New York Times*, 21 December 2003.

14 'Shine Wears off "Happy New Era" for Kenyans': *Daily Telegraph*, 30 December 2003.

15 'Envoy's Dressing Down Over Kenya Corruption Claim': Chris Munnion, *Daily Telegraph*, 15 July 2004.

16 'Greed and Corruption Rife in Kenya as Beleaguered Watchdog Resigns': *Washington Post*, 20 February 2005.

17 'President Goes to Bed as Kenya Declines': Adrian Blomfield, *Daily Telegraph*, 16 February 2005.

18 'African Union and Nepad Should Rein in the Tyrants':

Makau Mutua, *New York Times*, 22 August 2004.

CHAPTER 8

1 *Zimbabwe: From Impunity to Accountability*: Redress Trust (London), March 2004: www.redress.org
2 *Perceptions of the Official Opposition – Encouraging a Change in Political Consciousness in Zimbabwe*: speech by Morgan Tsvangirai to the South African Institute of International Affairs (Jan Smuts House, University of the Witwatersrand), 25 January 2005.
3 *The Private Sector, Political Elites and Underdevelopment in Sub-Saharan Africa*: Moeletsi Mbeki, South African Institute of International Affairs (Johannesburg), 2 August 2004.
4 'Making Democracy a Mainstay': Mvemba Phezo Dizolele, *Washington Times*, 23 December 2004.
5 Amnesty International: public statement, AI Index: AFR 52/004/2004, issued 30 November 2004.
6 'Foes of Death Penalty Making Gradual Gains in Africa': Marc Lacey, *New York Times*, 20 October 2004.
7 *A Thousand Suns*: Dominique Lapierre. London: Simon & Schuster UK Ltd, 1999.
8 *Country Reports on Human Rights Practices, 2004*: Bureau of Democracy, Human Rights and Labor, US State Department (Washington DC), February 2005.
9 Bennett was sentenced to fifteen months with hard labour, of which three months were suspended. *Roy Bennett, A Record of Political Persecution*: Derek Matyszak. Harare: Self-published, January 2005. For more information, see www.freeroybennett.com
10 These and other allegations levelled at the MDC are covered in detail in my previous book, *The Battle for Zimbabwe.*
11 Lyrics reproduced with written permission from Clem Tholet's widow, Jean.

Bibliography

Africa Insight Vol. 17, No. 4, 1987, edited by Richard Cornwell. The Africa Institute, Pretoria.

Amnesty International. *Policing to Protect Human Rights.* London: Amnesty International Publications, 2004.

Becker, Peter. *Path of Blood.* London: Longmans, 1962.

Blair, David. *Degrees in Violence.* London: Continuum Books, 2002.

Bulpin, TV. *To the Banks of the Zambezi.* Johannesburg: Thomas Nelson & Sons, 1965.

Chan, Stephen. *Robert Mugabe: A Life of Power and Violence.* London: Tauris, 2003.

Fothergill, Roland. *Mirror over Rhodesia.* Johannesburg: The Argus Printing and Publishing Company, 1984.

Gourevitch, Philip. *We Wish to Inform You That Tomorrow We Will Be Killed With Our Families: Stories from Rwanda.* New York: Farrar, Straus and Giroux, 1998.

Grace, John, and John Laffin. *Fontana Dictionary of Africa Since 1960.* London: Fontana Press, 1991.

Hill, Geoff. *The Battle for Zimbabwe.* Cape Town: Zebra Press, 2003.

Hoess, Rudolf. *Commandant of Auschwitz.* London: Weidenfeld & Nicholson, 1959.

Hudson, Miles. *Triumph or Tragedy.* London: Hamish Hamilton, 1981.

International Crisis Group. *Blood and Soil: Land, Politics and Conflict Prevention in Zimbabwe and South Africa.* Brussels: ICG, 2004.

Judd, Denis. *Empire.* London: HarperCollins, 1996.

Matyszak, Derek. *Roy Bennett, A Record of Political Persecution 2000–2005.* Harare, published privately, 2005.

Meldrum, Andrew. *Where We Have Hope.* London: John Murray 2004.

Meredith, Martin. *Robert Mugabe: Power, Plunder and Tyranny in Zimbabwe.* Johannesburg: Jonathan Ball, 2002.

———. *The First Dance of Freedom.* London: Hamish Hamilton, 1984.

Power, Samantha. *A Problem from Hell: America in the Age of Genocide.* London: Flamingo, 2002.

Today's News Today. Johannesburg: The Argus Printing and Publishing Company, 1956.

US State Department. *Report on Zimbabwe 2004.* Washington DC: Bureau of Democracy, Human Rights and Labor.

Zimbabwe: From Impunity to Accountability. London: The Redress Trust, 2004.

Index